REPORT FROM ROME

Report from Rome

On the First Session of the Vatican Council

YVES CONGAR, O.P.

CHRISTIAN LIVING SERIES

GEOFFREY CHAPMAN

THIS BOOK WAS FIRST PUBLISHED IN FRANCE, BY LES EDITIONS DU CERF, IN 1963, UNDER THE TITLE *Vatican II, Le Concile au Jour le Jour*. THE ENGLISH TRANSLATION IS BY A. MANSON. © TRANSLATION, 1963, GEOFFREY CHAPMAN LTD.

MADE AND PRINTED IN GREAT BRITAIN BY CHARLES BIRCHALL. & SONS LTD., LIVERPOOL AND LONDON. NIHIL OBSTAT : BERNADUS PATTEN, S.T.D., CENS. LIB.; IMPRIMATUR : DIONYSIUS MCDONNELL, VIC. GEN., LIVERPOLII, DIE 16A JULII, 1963.

Contents

Documents

Chapter 1

Leading up to the Second Vatican Council. Principal dates to remember

January, 1959. John XXIII, as he himself has told us, was first inspired to call a Council.

25 *January,* 1959. The pope told a group of eighteen cardinals in St Paul's Outside the Walls that he intended to summon a Council. That evening the Vatican issued a communiqué: 'The Holy Father does not envisage that the aim of the Council is only to procure the spiritual good of the Christian people; it is also to be an invitation to the separated communities to join in the search for unity.'

29 *January,* 1959. The cardinals of the world were asked to express their opinion of the pope's intention.

27 *April,* 1959. In a broadcast speech the pope asked the Catholics of the world to pray for the Council.

27 *May,* 1959 (*Pentecost*). The inauguration of the 'ante-preparatory phrase'. This was to last until 1 May, 1960. It would enable the suggestions for the Council, sent in by the bishops and universities, to be sorted out.

5 *June,* 1960. John XXIII created ten Commissions and

three Secretariats to prepare the Schemas to be submitted to the Council.

14 *November,* 1960. Solemn opening of the work of preparation. The pope explained to the members of the Commissions and Secretariats the general direction he wished
the Council to take.

The year 1961 was almost entirely taken up by the work
of the Commissions and Secretariats.

Christmas, 1961. John XXIII signed the bull *Humanae
salutis* which declared that the Council would be opened
in 1962, the precise date to be settled later. It was in fact
11 October.

11 *June,* 1962. Final session of the Central Commission.
The previous day, which was the Feast of Pentecost, the
pope had said: 'The Church, which is about to hold a
Council, rejects nothing that is of value and beauty in the
world today ... She wants to help and love all the men
of our time.'

6 *September,* 1962. A *motu proprio* from the pope decreed
the standing orders for the Council.

Chapter 2

The theological significance of the Council[1]

THE TRENDS WHICH HAVE LED UP TO THE SECOND Vatican Council are significant. In the fourth century Arianism, and in the sixteenth the Reformation, produced a crisis in the Catholic mind which in each case culminated in a Council. The situation today is different. Today, the scrutiny of the Church comes from a world which is asking the Church to enter with it into an authentic discussion of Jesus Christ. The crisis is apostolic and missionary. For in our time the gospel has to be proclaimed to a world in which one person out of every four is Chinese, two out of every three have not enough to eat, one out of every three lives under a communist regime, one Christian out of every two is not a Catholic. The gospel has to be proclaimed to a world where the energies of hope and the need for better things are in danger of becoming satisfied simply by the search for that comfort which technical invention can provide.

[1]This chapter was originally published in *Le Monde*, 6 September, 1962.

*In the twentieth century one particular dogma is at
stake: belief in the world to come.*

In the preface to his *Controversies* (about 1586),
Bellarmine spoke of a procession of heresies, attacking one
by one the articles of the Creed: Marcionism and Mani-
cheeism had disputed the article on the one God, the
creator of the goodness of things visible and invisible. In
the fourth century Arianism had attacked the divinity of
Christ and the mystery of the Triune God. The Christological heresies had struck at the root of the truth of the
Incarnation. From the ninth century onwards the East was
in conflict with the West over the procession of the Holy
Ghost. In his own days, said Bellarmine, it was the dogma
of the Church, one, holy, catholic and apostolic that had
come under fire from the Reformers. Four hundred years
have passed since that time. We are late comers, and the
only thing left for us to corrode is belief in eternal life and
the resurrection of the body. Atheistic communism and
materialist technology—which is not a monopoly of
Russia—has made this its special work and offers a religion
of earthly security and comfort that has no need of belief
in another life.

The West on trial.

Criticism of the West, with which the historical
development of Christianity seems to have been involved
(at least if in 'the West' we include part of the Middle East
and the extensions of Europe across the Atlantic), is another relevant trend. Wherever missions have had the

appearance of being bound up with the West they have been under a more or less serious handicap. The creation of indigenous hierarchies scarcely scratches the surface of the problem of native expression in worship and belief. At the present time there is an upsurge of new nationalistic movements. Yet often in countries in the same part of the world, a community of feeling and a common approach to problems is to be found, and groups whose unity lies somewhere midway between the national and the world-wide are tending to be formed. A conference of the bishops of Latin America already exists; the bishops of the Far East met together in Manila in October 1958. The Council may possibly set up continental or quasi-continental bodies, e.g. the bishops of the black races of Africa, and of the Churches of the Far East. This is only one aspect of the complex theological and practical problems that arise from the relations between the local episcopates and the Roman curia.

New circumstances in ecumenical relations.

The ecumenical movement is the third contemporary trend which has bearing upon the Council. Previous Councils had been concerned to exclude heretics: Arius and Nestorius were condemned or exiled; Luther was excommunicated. But this time heretics have been invited to the Council. At the Vatican Council there will be observers (or, in the expression used in Rome, 'official delegates') from the other Christian communities. It is true that at the council of Florence, Greek Orthodox Christians came to Rome and discussed, on equal footing, articles of belief that were dogmas for Catholics (1438-39). It is also true that Protestants were invited to explain their position at the Council of Trent; but, in the event, only a handful arrived and these were not seriously representative. Again, it is true that the Orthodox and, later, the Anglicans and Protestants, were invited to come to the Council of 1869: the former, in order to be united to the Holy See, the latter to expound their difficulties and to hear the answer made to them. The psychological atmosphere, however, was one of competition and controversy and did not favour a dialogue. Not one separated Christian formally attended the First Vatican Council.

Today relations have altered. This does not mean that either side is considering concessions; the Orthodox and the Protestants are no more inclined to make concessions than the Catholics are. What has happened is that the conflict of dogma has come to be approached in a less controversial spirit and with a sense of its historical origins which has smoothed many rough edges and produced a new spirit of prayer and friendship. A great deal of what is central and essential is common to both parties, and this fact now dictates the way in which the whole position can be considered. Of course it would be fanciful to expect immediate decisions to be taken about union. It is not, however, fanciful to hope for mutual discussion that might well pave the way for decisive contacts on certain matters. If a beginning is made in this direction, who can tell where it will end? And if the impetus is ultimately from God, who can say categorically where the division between the impossible and the possible lies?

Whichever of these major trends is considered, the point at issue is always the relationship between the Church and others. Today's basic problems are of this kind. It is not a matter of steadying the Catholic mind in face of internal dangers, but of adapting the Church to the world with which she is involved, because to it she has been sent. It seems certain that the Council will be primarily apostolic and pastoral, and that even its theological declarations will have this character. Such points of doctrine as may be considered or developed will be those which concern evangelical or pastoral relations with others. This may well prove to be the initial theological aspect of the significance of the Council.

The restoration of collegial power in the Church.

In the view of the present writer, the second and equally important aspect is the simple fact that a general Council has been summoned and is about to meet.

For Catholicism, the nineteenth century was a century of restoration, marked by the rise of the papacy to a predominant position. The century had begun in ruins; the French Revolution and the Empire had destroyed or overthrown almost all the social structures which had guaranteed the Church's power. Pius VI had died in the exile to which he had been banished by the republican soldiers; Pius VII survived an equally brutal exile, but his power was minimal. It was, however, from this lowest point of descent that the movement of return began. Joseph de Maistre, with resounding eloquence, acted as its prophet. But whilst he exalted the papacy he had no sympathy for and little understanding of the community of the Church as such. In 1817, he wrote: 'The most that is possible for the pope; the least possible for the Council.' 'Where is the need for an ecumenical Council, when the pillory will do the work?' The future was to bring a denial of his views from the Vatican, but was also to bring him satisfaction, for those years coincided with the extraordinary growth of the papacy in prestige, spiritual power, and function in the Church. Pius IX, Leo XIII, Pius X, Pius XI and Pius XII: between them a hundred and twenty years of great pontificates punctuated by encyclicals and allocutions which bishops and periodicals had simply to transmit and discuss. The mind of the whole Church took shape from its Roman centre; it might be said that the whole Church looked to Rome as its centre of consciousness.

Due emphasis is restored to the Church.

Möhler and, above all, Newman explained this extraordinary growth in the exercise of the papal magisterium by the no less extraordinary upsurge of rationalism which rejected all control, even the control of divine authority, and doubted or questioned everything. This made it necessary for the Church to react by affirming sanity and certitude. Möhler's and Newman's outlook differed from de Maistre's; and they considered that this concentration of authority in one voice alone was excessive; yet Newman wrote: 'Considered in its fullness, this power is as huge as the gigantic evil that provoked it ... it is a supreme and amazing power sent on earth to combat and control a gigantic evil.'

Now, suddenly, in our time, authority has been given back to the Church. Indeed, the Church had never lost it; and we have no intention of setting the Church and the papacy in opposition to each other. But it is a fact that today the century-long, one-sided development of papal authority has been as it were suspended, and initiative has been restored to the Church. So the opportunity arises for a better understanding of a feature essential to the Church, but more or less submerged for nearly five hundred years—the corporate and collegial character of her inmost life.

The collegial authority of the bishops and the primacy of the pope.

In reality this characteristic has never been lost. At the period of his greatest power, the pope still nominated bishops. He could not preside over the Church unless their 'college' presided with him. Even the Roman central administration worked by means of Commissions and information services to which the whole world contributed. But a Council is a different matter. It presupposes and expresses the life of the whole body. The bishops attend it, not indeed as separable from the pope, but as possessing an authority not emanating from his: they are the successors of the 'college' of the apostles that held its power not from Peter, but from Christ who chose this way to construct his Church. By divine right, the Church entails both a Petrine primacy and a 'college' of bishops. No doubt one of the theological tasks of the coming Council will be to reaffirm this.

This could prove momentous from an ecumenical point of view. A number of dissident communions (Orthodox, Anglicans to some extent, and even some Lutherans) attach great importance to the episcopate, but all of them pull up short before a papal power which in their view is absolutist and monarchical. Again, they all show a marked concern for the Church as the community of Christians and for the local assemblies, each of which reproduces the mystery expressed by the whole Church. This is one of the reasons why John XXIII's initiative, which for three years has been reinforced daily by countless gestures and words which spring from an evangelical simplicity and goodness of heart, has met with such profound response from other Christians.

What is a Council?

We will conclude this outline of the theological signific-ance of the Council by three remarks concerning the nature of Councils as such. It is essential not to be de-ceived by the resemblance between a Council and other human gatherings, which springs from the fact that it is necessarily constituted by men and has to use human methods. A Council has a specific nature which we should respect:

1. A Council is an assembly.

When Pius IX was considering the formulation of the dogma of the Immaculate Conception of the Mother of God (1854), and Pius XII that of her bodily Assump-tion, both of them proceeded to consult the entire Catholic episcopate several years in advance. This method has been described as 'a council held in writing', but here the emphasis does not fall on the word 'council'. A consulta-tion might take place in writing, but a Council is a different thing from a papal consultation and the difference in the procedure used by the two above-mentioned popes and by

John XXIII is a confirmation of the theological significance which we have already discussed of the very fact that
there is going to be a council. A Council is not even a papal
consultation that involves an actual gathering of the consultants. In every case, it is essential that it should be a
meeting in person of the bishops of the world (or of a
region, if it is a local council). The precise theological
point involved is that of presence. To put it better, it is
a coming together, an assembly in common, a fraternal
meeting in concord, with a view, first to seek God's help
and enlightenment and then to reach decisions. A saying
in the gospels provides the clue, and it has in fact been
invoked on innumerable occasions: 'Where two or three
are gathered together in my name, I am there in the midst
of them' (Matt. 18:20).

2. *A Council is a phenomenon peculiar to the Church.*

A Council is not simply a meeting of human beings. It is
a manifestation proper to the Church alone. Marriage in
church is a different reality from marriage before a regis-
trar; a third person enters into the contract together with
the partners, making the contract a sacrament. Similarly,
the Church, in St Paul's phrase, is the Body of Christ;
she is incorporated in him and he is above her as her Head.
In like manner, a Council is held in God's presence, and
he takes a supremely active part in it. Whether it is Christ
who is invoked and whose presence is symbolized by an
open Bible on the altar (this Council, it is said, will use
one of the finest and most venerable manuscripts of Holy
Scripture, the *Codex Vaticanus*), or whether it is the Holy
Spirit who is invoked—Councils are traditionally said to

be 'lawfully assembled in the Holy Spirit'—the two different invocations present no difficulty to anyone acquainted with the theology of the relationship between the
Holy Spirit and Christ. The essential thing is that presence, which is active and decisive. At the Vatican Council
there will be some 2500 bishops—exact numbers can be
obtained from the newspapers—AND the Holy Spirit!

This does not prevent a Council from being human,
very human, sometimes all too human. As with the entire
course of the history of salvation—a fact keenly appreciated by the Jews—Councils are utterly human and historical events, but they are also events in which and
through which God, faithful to his covenant, achieves his
purpose. After all, scripture is like this from end to end,
although God's active presence in it has that special
quality we call 'inspiration', which marks it off from the
ordinary assistance promised to the Church.

3. A Council is a celebration.

The second feature of a Council entails and explains the
third. A Council is not merely *held* like a conference; it is
celebrated. It will open, on 11 October, with worship. The
splendour of this opening, a little archaic perhaps, will
provide sensational photographs and reports for the press
and, unfortunately, for television. It may not be as magni-
ficent as the coronation of the Queen but, in any case, its
reality must be looked for on a different level. A day of
fasting will doubtless precede it. God is to be implored; a
sacred action carried out; an entry into the divine presence effected; brethren are to meet in solemn worship. In
short, it is something specifically Christian.

Chapter 3

The Church celebrates the opening of the Council

11 October, 1962

An occasion for ear and eye

ST PETER'S SEEMS TO HAVE BEEN BUILT JUST FOR *this*. It was a fascinating spectacle of colour, in which gold and red predominated. Everything gleamed and sparkled in the brilliant light of the arc-lamps. The décor had the somewhat theatrical spirit of the Baroque: a certain chilliness in the solemnity. The seating arrangements were eloquent of the history of the Church. The pope's throne was set apart, a self-sufficient presidential power, facing the vast nave. It was set in front of the altar, above the Tomb of St Peter: *Petrus ipse,* it is Peter himself. On the right hand side where the nave begins, below the Tomb which is at the crossing of the transepts, there is a statue of St Peter dressed in the style of Boniface VIII, with cape and triple tiara: *Papa ipse,* it is the pope. Facing this statue, the red seats of the cardinals were placed in ascending rows. Then, on each side of the nave, divided by a wide central corridor, the benches for archbishops and bishops, hung with green, stretched opposite each other as far as the entrance to the nave, near the gate of the basilica.

The Eastern patriarchs occupied the first seats, in front of the archbishops. There is something not quite right about that. The solution to the problem of giving the patriarchs of Alexandria, Antioch and Jerusalem a position corresponding to the apostolic dignity of their sees has not been found (has it really been sought?).

The diplomatic delegations made their entry in succession, accompanied by Swiss guards with raised halberds. Eastern pomp and Renaissance pomp combined within the immense basilica. Nothing could be more visually satisfying. It has often been said that the Jewish people, the people of the Word and the Bible, were characterized by hearing; the Greeks, a people of light and of clearly defined forms, by sight. At this stage, only the eyes were satisfied, and everyone was trying to *see*. In a moment, there would be plenty to hear, but only in the sense of musical sound and not of Biblical utterance. When the bishops in procession had slowly entered and taken their place and, last of all the pope, mass began. But the mass was not accompanied by any liturgy of the Word, and instead of the immense priestly assembly taking part, at least by singing the Creed, we assisted at a mass sung by the choir of the Sistine Chapel, i.e. by professional singers. Has the liturgical movement come to a halt before the gates of bronze? Hundreds of bishops shared this regret at the absence of a common celebration when, in their own dioceses, they have been doing everything to initiate priests and people into it. As for my Protestant friends, who do not share this eastern passion for colour, what must they have felt?[1]

---

[1] With regard to the celebration of the liturgy at the Council it should be mentioned that the closing mass on 8 December was sung by the Fathers, as the result of a petition signed by a great number of them. The initiative for this came from the Spanish bishops.

'The whole Church has assembled'

And yet the whole Church was here, together at the heart of its sacred unity and apostolic catholicity. What fervent prayer was rising at that moment from this heart which is ancient and ever new? Its fervour was caught in the prayer *Adsumus*,[1] which is thought to have been composed by St Isidore for the fourth Council of Toledo (633), and which is recited before each session of the Council. Before each session every morning, prayer is addressed to St Peter in union with that immense prayer for the Council which is being offered all round the world, beseeching God in a common supplication.

The Holy Father made a fairly general speech[2] which has received different interpretations, especially in the sub-headings the press gave to it. The *Osservatore Romano* used the headlines: 'The Council's main purpose: to defend and promote doctrine', 'Why errors should be suppressed'. *Le Monde* said: 'John XXIII advocates the "methods of enquiry of modern thought".' Then it quoted the words with which the discourse began: 'Our duty is not only to preserve the precious treasure of the patrimony of the faith, as if we were concerned only with the past, but to set ourselves with determination and fearlessness to the task our age demands and thus continue in the direction which the Church has followed for twenty centuries.' *Petre, duc in altum!* A large number of bishops did, in fact, consider that this passage was an indication of the Holy Father's wish to see the Council not merely reiterate past

[1] Cf. Document I, p. 95
[2] Cf. Document II, p. 97

gains but open the way of the gospel in the world of the twentieth century. It was said that, in this spirit, the Council should open with a kind of Message to the World, a message foreshadowed by the pope's admirably Christian discourse of 11 September.[1]

A Council alert to the needs of the modern world.

In the past few days we have read right through, and followed the thread of, all the speeches in which the pope has spoken about the Council since he first mentioned it on 25 January, 1959. A passage from the one in which, as bishop of the See, he opened the Synod of Rome on 24 January, 1960 seems worthy of special consideration. He recalled that the first Synod or Council held by the Apostles, about A.D. 50, constituted a permanent ideal and criterion for the conciliary life of the Church. He observed that two things were particularly striking about that synod:

1. Its members heard Paul and Barnabas tell of the conversion of the Gentiles and this caused much joy among the brethren (Acts 11:3). The coming Council will therefore be missionary. But who, among its members, will play the part of Paul and Barnabas? Who will define for us the direction the gospel should take and its specific attraction for the Gentiles of the twentieth century?

2. That Synod considered, and it was an urgent question for the Church at that time, what conditions the Gentiles must observe in order to become Christians in a Church whose first Council was composed of converts

Cf. Document III, p. 106

from Judaism. It was decided that neither circumcision nor the Law of Moses should be imposed on them. The Council, therefore, will offer a welcome to the Gentiles of the modern world, to the people knocking on the baptistry door; the assembly will make the adaptations necessary to open up for today's Gentiles a broader avenue of approach to the faith.

Chapter 4

Outline of events,
11 October—20 October, 1962

11 *October*. In the evening two observers from the Russian Orthodox Church arrived in Rome from Moscow.

12 *October*. John XXIII received the representatives of the diplomatic missions in the Sistine Chapel.

John XXIII added fourteen additional experts to the 201 he had previously nominated. He received the special diplomatic missions in the Sistine Chapel.

13 *October*. Meeting of the first general Congregation summoned to elect the 160 members of the ten Commissions. It ended after half an hour; Cardinal Liénart, supported by Cardinal Frings, proposed that the first voting should be postponed until Tuesday, 16 October, so that the Fathers of the Council might have time to become better acquainted and to reflect on the candidates. The proposal was accepted unanimously.

A meeting of the French bishops in the afternoon.

John XXIII received thirty-nine non-Catholic observers in the hall of the Consistory and journalists in the Sistine Chapel.

14 *October*. A further meeting of the French bishops. In

the following days other national episcopates also held meetings. At a press conference, the Abbé Haubtmann, director of the Religious Information Bureau of the French bishops, emphasized that the French bishops wanted at all costs to avoid the formation of pressure groups.

15 *October*. John XXIII received bishop F. Colson, the observer-delegate of the Methodists.

Mgr Cassien, a bishop of the Russian Orthodox Church, rector of the Institute of Saint-Sergius in Paris, accepted an invitation to attend the Council. With Mgr Antoine of Geneva, he will be the second orthodox bishop to attend.

Cardinal Bea held a reception for the non-Catholic observers.

The pope nominated four under-secretaries to the Council.

Meeting of the Eastern patriarchs with Mgr Méouchi.

16 *October*. Second general Congregation: the Fathers had until 6 p.m. to hand in their votes for the Commissions. The sorting of votes (430,000) lasted until Saturday 20th, the date of the third general Congregation.

The pope had a lengthy meeting with the ten members of the Council of Presidency.

Second meeting of the non-Catholic observers at the Secretariat for Unity.

18 *October*. The pope nominated Cardinal Wyszynski, the primate of Poland, as the seventh member of the Secretariat for special matters. He also nominated a fifth under-secretary to the Council.

Meeting of the ten members of the Council of Presidency.

18-21 *October*. Various meetings of national or regional

episcopates to prepare the Schema on the liturgy. The African bishops (indigenous and missionary), who have formed a Secretariat with Cardinal Rugambwa (Tanganyika) as president, held an important meeting with the French bishops and, at a further meeting, Canon Martimort (France) gave them an address on the liturgy which he had previously given to the French bishops.

20 *October.* Third general Congregation presided over by Cardinal Liénart. As the result of a change, allowed by John XXIII, in article 39 of the regulations (which had required an absolute majority) the sixteen candidates who had gained the greatest number of votes for each Commission were elected. The names of the members elected for seven of the ten Commissions were published.

Chapter 5

The Council begins to function

THE FIRST GENERAL CONGREGATION WAS TO BE devoted to the election by 2500 bishops of 160 of their members: 16 for each of the 10 Commissions; the number on each Commission was to be brought up to 24 by the pope's nomination of 8 more bishops. This choice of 160 names by 2500 bishops involved a total of 400,000 votes! We have seen that Cardinal Liénart, supported by Cardinal Frings in the name of the German, Dutch and Austrian bishops, proposed that the election be deferred and preparation made for it by the meeting, and if possible the agreement, of the 42 episcopal conferences already in existence. This suggestion was at once welcomed with applause.

On this matter, the newspaper *France-soir* was guilty of frivolity, discourtesy, and even downright dishonesty. Its Paris edition printed a headline in large type: 'French bishops in revolt at the council.' Had this been a session of the United Nations, would the paper have dared to act in this way? Is frivolity to be tolerated with reference to matters and to an assembly which are of such absolute gravity? There is not an atom of truth in what is suggested by this headline, an implication which damages those causes we most cherish. On the contrary, the French bishops have constantly shown their desire to make contact with all the other episcopates. To achieve this they appointed set times and places where a large number of them might be accessible to all comers. They have declared all their meetings open to all other bishops. No partisanship exists among them, still less any spirit of coterie, intrigue or nationalism.

The first conciliar act.

Cardinal Liénart's gesture was, however, of wide significance and largely determined the later development of the Council. *It was the first conciliary act:* not in the trivial sense of some routine act of ordinary Council business, not in the inadmissible and excluded sense of any kind of 'conciliar gamesmanship', but in the sense of an assembly freely deliberating and reaching a decision. It indicated the general will of the bishops to deal with matters and come to decisions on their own account, discarding even the shadow of prefabricated opinion or of backstairs guidance.

There can be no doubt that the Holy Father concurs in this. He may be absent in body but he is present in mind and heart at every initiative taken by the council as a whole.

The weight of numbers.

One fact that was to press heavily on the labours of the Council became evident from the very first meetings devoted to the election of the two-thirds of the episcopal

Commissions: this was the excessive number of participants, 2500 bishops! Looking ahead, it was calculated that the least amendment put forward in general congregation, discussed in Commission, re-examined several days afterwards in another general congregation, then again discussed and finally voted on, would require at least twenty-five hours, spread over two or three weeks. But the shortest of the Schemas put forward by the preparatory Commissions would certainly provoke fifty or a hundred amendments, perhaps even more . . .

What was to be done? Sociologists distinguish several kinds of assembly, whose nature is determined by numbers. Once a certain size has been passed there is a change in scope and character; a community becomes a 'public' or an 'audience'. A mass of 2500 persons, each of whom must have an inalienable right to make himself heard, is so crushing that it is difficult to see how it can be lifted.

It has been said that the pope, conscious of this difficulty, had envisaged this first session as an occasion for prospecting, so that the possible might be distinguished from the impossible, the inconveniences of this or that procedure ascertained, and rules whose useful or obstructive elements could be known only from experience corrected. When an engine has been put together it is tested and kept running until it betrays its inherent weaknesses. In the case of the Council, it would only be in the second session that the more difficult questions would be considered, and the reformed rules introduced.[1]

---

[1] It had been intended that the second session of the Council should open shortly after Easter, in May 1963. This date was later amended to the autumn of 1963.

The bishops get to know each other.

This way of looking at the first session receives support from another point of view also. The bishops soon came to realize that outside their own national groups they had little knowledge of one another. Their first fortnight was spent in seeing each other, becoming acquainted, and in giving body and movement to that 'horizontal catholicity' about which Cardinal Feltin spoke and of which readers of *Informations catholiques internationales* are well aware.

The discovery, which the bishops made and saw in action, of an organized and organically interrelated world episcopate, may well prove to be one of the most enduring and promising results of the Council. The episcopate is already organized in many countries, since forty-two episcopal conferences do exist. But this is not so everywhere. The episcopate might also develop—here and there it has already done so, e.g. in Latin America—on a continental scale, or in order to embrace great regions like the Far East, Africa, Western Europe. It would of course be foolish to use phrases like 'the Church of the Six' or indeed the Church of the Seven or the Fourteen. *The Church is a communion:* this is the title of an admirable book by P. J. Hamer just published by Editions du Cerf in Paris.)[1] That is why we speak of a world-wide episcopate, organically interrelated. What we mean is that it is conscious of forming a single body whose organs maintain an active and regular interchange and all work together to produce a life that is unique, vital, and

[1] English translation to be published by Geoffrey Chapman in Autumn 1964.

rich in content: all of which presupposes that the organs necessary for this purpose exist.

The collegiate character of the episcopate.

During the last three years there has been much talk of 'episcopal collegiality'. By this is meant the fact that bishops succeed as a body to the Apostolic College as a body, Peter being the visible head of this body; that together they are responsible for the whole, even though in ordinary affairs each bishop has personal charge of some definite section of that whole. This idea of collegiality— its dogmatic basis is both profound and certain—seems to correspond to a need of the contemporary Church whose mission is to the contemporary world. It is very probable that one of the results of the Council will be to bring this home to the minds of all its members, to bring it into a clearer theological light, and to express it in new ways, written into the organization of the great body of the Church.

The observers are there.

Tears came to my eyes when I met the observers for the first time. Of course their presence has to become effective, and everything still remains to be done. Naturally they will have moments of boredom, dryness and irritation. But the essential point has been gained: *they are there*. The status assigned to them is generous and straight forward. Exactly like 'the experts', they attend the general Congregations, in which the bishops speak their minds, and if invited or authorized by the president they may be present at one or other of the working sessions of the Commissions. They have not the right to speak, but they may send in observations in writing. They are perfectly free to inform the Communions they represent of proceedings.

This juridical position carries its own implications. But in practice the role of the observers, whether they are delegates or have been specially invited, will be what they make of it. Or rather, as is the case with every dialogue, the two parties will mutually affect each other by their approach, their reserve, their withdrawal and their general feelings. If matters go well—and the Secretariat for Unity is doing its best to ensure that they will—the observers may meet a considerable number of the Council Fathers and the experts. Who can calculate the influence which frank and disinterested private conversations might have over the direction in which certain debates develop? This is all the more likely since the pervading environment is one of genuine prayer, which truly does constitute an atmosphere palpably ecumenical. May God be praised!

Rome, 18 October

Chapter 6

Exploration: the Council
takes shape

THE FIRST NOTE MAKES OR MARS THE CONCERT. IT immediately reveals the quality of the performer. At the Council this first note was the Message to the World[1] which on 20 October was approved by the practically unanimous vote of the 2439 Fathers.

The Fathers of the Council showed that they were resolved to produce that 'reasonable exposition of the Church' postulated by the pope, in the sense of a Church looking outwards towards men and being present in the world. The Council will be resolutely pastoral. This, in fact, is what it has become, confining its attention to practical problems and showing little interest in theology as such. But, in our time, theologians themselves, although not of course abandoning theology, do not elaborate it in isolation from human life.

On this point, as on many others, a comparison with the First Vatican Council reveals more points of difference than of resemblance. The theologians of 1869–70 lived behind the walls of technical theology. Those who were concerned

[1] Cf. Document III, p. 106.

with the composition of the conciliar decrees were mainly academic personalities, teaching in Rome. Today the theologians who matter have abandoned the scholastic form which depended for its success on Latin formulae. Their work is no less technical, but in its sources, documentation and material it is more involved in human life. It tries to investigate and illuminate the main problems of that life from the point of view of scripture, tradition and reflection, taking these as its point of departure. One has only to think of Guardini, K. Rahner, M-D Chenu, H. de Lubac, Schillebeeckx. . . .

The council gets its wind.

It seems that little work was done during the previous fortnight. Of the 73 Schemas produced by the preparatory Commissions only one had been considered and then only the 'introduction' and first two chapters had been discussed. There are eight chapters in all. The suggested amendments have to be inspected by the Commission and then sent back to the assembly to be voted on. At this rate, an archbishop said to me, it is not only we who will not see the end, our successors also will be dead before it finishes. . . . The Presidency and the general Secretariat are busy trying to discover a speedier way of proceeding. It is possible, however, that the time spent was necessary for the bishops whose previous interests had precluded an acquaintance with some of the ideas to be discussed, and that this was their opportunity to appreciate the existence of such ideas, inform themselves about them, acquire the necessary familiarity with them. . . .

On any hypothesis, one thing at least has been achieved:

the past fortnight has begun to give the Council its definite form. Four main factors have emerged, to each of
which we shall devote a paragraph: the Commissions; the
appearance of internal tensions; the spirit of the Council;
the confirmation of a central issue.

The Commissions of the Council.

The Commissions have now been completed; the pope
has nominated the third of their members which he had
reserved to himself to appoint. Instead of nominating
eight, he has in fact selected nine, probably in order to
include the secretary of the corresponding Congregation
(for the Liturgy, Mgr Dante). The appointments made
by the pope have strengthened the conservative elements
(often identical with the Roman curia) in several Commissions. In the Commission on the Liturgy, the only one
at work for the moment, the President, Cardinal Larraona,
and the ninth member, Mgr Dante, are reputed to be
opposed not only to 'innovations', but also to any serious
adaptations. Thus, it is affirmed, a marked divergence may
show itself between the direction and will of the great
majority of the Council and that of the Commission. The
word 'majority' has, however, little relevance, for although
the votes of two-thirds are necessary for a proposition to
be accepted, one-third is sufficient for it to be turned down.

This hints at the possibility of some conflict between the
assembly and the Commissions. In the assembly the conservative elements might well be neutralized by the throng
of more dynamic pastors, but in the Commissions if they
do not dominate, they may at least gain practical control.
The assembly must therefore be careful not to allow itself

to be neutralized by the Commissions whose statutory role is to be its servants; it must overcome its own weariness and impatience, the temptation to be quit of the endless sessions of an interminable Council. If they fail in this, the Commissions might do the work, in a less desirable way, which the assembly had shown itself powerless to bring to a conclusion. It is even said that some are counting on this exhaustion, this impotence and desertion of the field, in order to gain control of a situation which a Council whose vigour was enduring would not have yielded to them.

Internal dissensions come to light.

The press has made much of divergent and even opposing opinions on the use of Latin or the vernacular tongue in the liturgy, which is certainly a very important issue —and also on two points which are of less passionate concern but are significant from a theological and even a pastoral point of view: (1) communion under two kinds (2) priestly concelebration in certain circumstances. For our part, we are definitely in favour of these three things. But we think that their doctrinal basis has been insufficiently considered. All three have, in fact, both practical aspects and doctrinal grounds. Very briefly, these are as follows:

1. *The use of the vernacular.*

The pastoral and practical utility is obvious. A colleague was preaching during Lent in a small town in the east of France, about 1927–29. One week he had to give a retreat for domestic servants. The instructions were timed for 5 p.m. The priest warned him: 'Very few will turn up; that is a time when they cannot come.' Should not a bishop tell his young priests on their ordination day: 'I am ordaining you to celebrate mass and I warn you: Few will turn up; the people cannot understand the language!' The dogmatic basis, if we are not mistaken, is this: the 'subject' of the liturgical celebration, i.e. the instrument of its performance, is not the clergy (the ministers ordained for this purpose) alone, but the community in union with its priest, the *plebs tua sancta* of the Canon of the Mass. A whole line of theology which has been developed during the last twenty years is relevant here; the theology of the baptized as consecrated and spiritually priests;[1] the theology of the Christian community and of the active role of the laity in all the activities of the Church.

2. *Communion in both kinds.*

Practical considerations would be rather against this. Its general observance would certainly considerably extend the time needed for the administering of Holy Communion, and would present other difficulties. But the Council has not been asked for its general practice. Communion in both kinds is envisaged only for certain definite occasions when the participation of God's people in his Alliance is verified

---

1 On this point we may mention a significant detail which, in its own way, springs from these 'tensions'. The *Osservatore Romano* of 1 November 1962 gave, in the official communique of the 11th general Congregation, a strange version in Italian of the following passage which appears in all the other versions:

To develop a realization of *a priesthood common* to all believers by virtue of the 'character' bestowed on them in baptism and confirmation.	La consapevolezza degli obblighi comuni (*common obligations*) a tutti i fedeli in virtù del carattere del Battesimo e della Cresima.

with particular intensity: ordinations, religious professions, nuptial masses (for the married couple only), masses celebrated after the baptism of an adult (for the newly baptized only). The doctrinal reasons in favour of this practice have no connection with the false idea, rightly condemned by the Councils of Florence and Trent, that communion in one kind only is incomplete. In fact it is precisely because this point of doctrine is absolutely unquestioned and everywhere accepted that the question of a very limited change in practice may again be raised. However limited, the change would be sufficient to show the importance of a *complete re-presentation* of the sacrifice. This re-presentation presupposes the two elements. It is essential to the Mass as such; its presence in communion would show more clearly the connection between the communion and the sacrifice.

3. Concelebration.

This also has only been requested (as regards the Latin rite) for certain definite cases, clearly listed and exclusive: congresses of priests; gatherings of the clergy with their bishop; pilgrimages; monastic community masses. At present, monks, living in common, share the same physical table . . . but not the Lord's! *Practical* reasons are particularly compelling for concelebration. But doctrinal reasons are equally obvious: the manifestation of the unity of the priesthood and the sacrifice under the supreme direction of the one high priest, Jesus Christ; the collegial character of the priesthood, as it is described by early writings in the Church (St Ignatius of Antioch) and in the liturgy.

On all these points and especially the first, which is of the greatest practical importance, there has arisen an attitude of opposition to all change, especially on the part of the old guard, which contrasts with an openness of mind which is very prevalent in the Council, although a good many would, it seems, be content with a middle position. The difference is not between innovators and traditionalists. Those who are willing to accept change welcome it for pastoral and missionary reasons, and also because the changes represent a return to authentic tradition. It is moving to see that the Eastern Christians, representatives of the most ancient and venerable traditions, are eager to support them. The difference is rather between those who feel self-sufficient and those who do not, or between the ministers of a Church wholly self-contained, mainly concerned with its own authority, legitimacy and prestige, sensitive to anything which may threaten its dominant position, and ministers of a Church-for-mankind. . . .

It is often suggested that the position taken up by a man is determined beforehand as the result of fundamental decisions imposed by his temperament and education, and that the arguments adduced are simply an ulterior justification of a position taken by instinct or from a sense of loyalty to social class. This may happen in many instances. It is certainly not true of a great number of bishops. We find entire episcopates changing, not so much as the result of the arguments put forward as in response to the general spirit and from contact with other episcopates from other continents and different horizons.

The spirit of the Council.

The spirit of the Council reflects the spirit of John

XXIII, which is a spirit of supernatural trust and optimism, of pastoral open-heartedness and humility, of kindliness and peace. Until now this spirit has undoubtedly been maintained. Everything must be done to prevent it from deteriorating. This would happen if normal and beneficial tensions should develop into parties, with their sterile cold or tepid war. The French bishops, aware of this, have tried to make contact between the various groups and have opened their meetings and their hospitality to all. May God preserve us from the spirit of contention, without detriment to firm convictions and their expression.

The Council is also in its own way an 'environment' which has its own significance and influence. Classical theology may have failed to estimate the concrete implications of the distinction between bishops gathered in Council and bishops scattered throughout the world. It is the same 'college,' but in two different states. The gathering as such has its own character and develops its own special potentiality. It provides an opportunity for a broad, spontaneous and uninhibited expansion of the human mind's instinct for mutual converse, for enrichment through contact and communication with others. This is realized or suspected by those who, in order to hinder this free intellectual intercourse, limit or eliminate its possibilities: totalitarian regimes controlled by police or suspicion; regimes which reduce men to isolated individuals by a system of oaths, secret decisions, displacement of populations. . . .

Within its frontiers, which are those of the Catholic world (represented by its bishops) and yet of the whole Christian world also (since there is free exchange of opinion with the observers, who attend all debates) the Council is, intrinsically, an agora or forum of the Christian spiritual Republic. Its prevailing spirit is that of freedom: freedom for those who consider that they have something worth saying to put forward their ideas. The cost of such freedom is the prolongation of sessions; thirty or forty speakers declaim in succession. This dragging progress has to be accepted. The price of freedom is always high, but the price is always relative to its value and therefore lower than the value itself which, in its own order, is absolute.

A central question: the episcopate.

It is becoming quite clear that the central question for the council concerns the episcopate. This has emerged in the present examination of the Schema on the Liturgy, where the function of episcopal conferences in the direct regulation of certain adaptations in the liturgy is mentioned as possible and, indeed, necessary, according to the needs of the various countries. The episcopate of Africa and Madagascar, with exciting territories to administer, is among the most developed and this has been one of the surprises of the Council. On several occasions, one of its bishops has spoken in the name of 299 of his colleagues and expressed their unanimous opinion.

There is another aspect which justifies the description of the Council as *the Council of the episcopate*. Canon F. Boulard has made a point which he considers to be self-evident. The Council of Trent gave rise to a new kind of bishop; the bishop as a feudal lord became a thing of the past; the pastoral bishop replaced him. St Charles Borromeo was the perfect example of this. The present Council is showing us that yet another kind of bishop is in the making: bishops alert to the world's problems and not merely administrators of the internal business of the Church as a clerical society. They will form an episcopate of the leaders of a Church which realizes that its work is concerned not only with the sacred and specialized affairs of religion but also with showing the world, the world as it is, secular and concerned with material development, the Christian and evangelical mind. For this secular world can only attain completion, can only secure peace, in Christ, the hope, the light, the divine centre of the universe.

Very many bishops are anxious that the Council should do for the episcopate what the first Council of the Vatican did for the papacy, i.e. define its function and authority. Fr Portal considered that the rights of bishops could 'only reach definition through time and custom' (cf. J. Guitton, *Dialogue avec les Précurseurs* p. 49). The time has come; custom is now a fully developed fact. Will the hoped-for decisions be made during the second session before or after Easter 1963, or will it be dealt with in the present session? We shall know perhaps before the end of the fortnight now beginning.

Rome, 2 November

Chapter 7

Outline of events,
21 October—15 November, 1962

From 21 *October to* 15 *November*: the chief work of the Council has been on the Schema prepared by the Commission on the Liturgy.

22 *October*: At the fourth general Congregation, presided over by Cardinal Gilroy, Archbishop of Sydney, two expositions of the liturgy were presented to the Fathers, one by Cardinal Larraona, the other by the very Reverend Father Antonelli. Immediately afterwards, and on the following day, 23 October, many criticisms of the Schema as a whole were made.

23 *October*–15 *November*: The foreword and the eight chapters of the Schema were examined by the Fathers, and provoked a number of questions.

14 *November*: First votes on: 'the guiding principles of the liturgical Schema which aim, with prudence and understanding, to make the different parts of the liturgy more alive and better adapted to present pastoral needs', and on the submission of amendments (nearly 2000) to the Commission.

Results of this vote:

For—	2162
Against—	46
Abstentions—	7

Further votes giving substantially the same results were registered on 17 *November*. During this same period considerable unofficial activity was observed with regard to the Schema on the Liturgy: press conference given by Mgr Van Bekkum, Archbishop of Ruteng (Indonesia); a conference given by Cardinal Lercaro to the Brazilian episcopate, and by Mgr Jenny, auxiliary Bishop of Cambrai, to French-speaking journalists.

Other events.

The Secretariat for Christian Unity, with Cardinal Bea as president, has been made into a conciliar Commission by papal decree, and hence has now the right to present the Schemas it may have prepared.

13 *November*: Cardinal Cicognani informs the Fathers that the pope has decided to introduce the name of St Joseph into the canon of the mass.

Chapter 8

The Liturgy as a starting point

The council is a celebration.

The Council is neither a parliament nor a conference, but a celebration. The early Councils may not have experienced such liturgical display. Every day at St Peter's the general Congregation begins with a dialogue mass,[1] during which the Sistine choir sings a few modest motets. All the bishops wear their liturgical vestments; purple soutane, rochet and mantella. After the mass the solemn enthronement of the gospels takes place. It is an intense moment, full of moving spiritual beauty. Slowly, between two acolytes bearing candles, one bishop moves up the central aisle to the altar, carrying an open book of the gospels (fine incunabula were chosen), whilst all the bishops, standing, sing the *Laudate,* with the refrain, *Christus Vincit* (Christ is the victor, Christ reigns, Christ rules!). Some days the Creed is chanted. The book of the gospels is put on the altar, on a golden support, between

---

[1] Unfortunately practically none of the successive celebrants have grasped the fact that a congregation of 2,500 will have a different pace from a single altar server: almost all rushed the prayers so that the *Gloria, Sanctus* and *Pater*, instead of having the moving dignity befitting such a throng, were hurried through in a way that was somewhat trying to those used to communal celebrations worthily performed.

lighted candles. The gospels preside over the council. Let them speak!

May this admirable sign of the Word not become a mere ceremony. It is my hope that when the book is opened a few verses will be read at the beginning of each congregation, chosen with reference to the subject of the day, and followed by two minutes silence.

For the Word of God seeks utterance and needs to be heard in silence.

Discussion of liturgical matters.

The laity were somewhat disappointed. The discussion was largely about specifically clerical problems, e.g. the breviary, and those problems that mattered most to the laity, for instance, marriage and penance (occupying a mere two lines in the Schema) were considered solely from the point of view of their liturgical form, i.e. their external celebration, whereas they were interested in so many other aspects of these subjects. This happened because the clergy have been educated in the scholastic method, and Rome loves the customary procedure above all things. In this case the matters under discussion were not considered as a whole, but from the precise aspect mentioned in the agenda.

This is very proper, and yet there is no use hiding the fact that taken to the extreme this procedure will prejudice a fully pastoral discussion. Pastoral work means activity in the real world and therefore must synthesize. Division into well-defined spheres of influence makes analysis easier and fosters juridical clarity, of which we have many examples here. But when the work of analysis and abstraction has been done, the practical regrouping of conclusions into a synthesis must never be neglected.

The problems of the breviary have led the Fathers to consider once again the subject of episcopal conferences and their authority. This is a constantly recurring issue. The Council cannot avoid a thorough and positive study of it. One of the results will be the formation of an episcopate, organized according to the different stages of its development, that really does govern the Church of God.

St Joseph in the Canon of the Mass.

On 13 November, while the Council was still discussing the liturgical year and its feasts, it was informed that the pope, in response to a petition from four hundred bishops, had inserted the name of St Joseph in the Canon of the Mass.

Reactions were varied. A Protestant observer said to Oscar Cullmann: 'You have published a Christology, now you must compose a Josephology.' Cullmann replied: 'That has already been done; I have seen a fat volume with this title in the Gregorian university.'

There was also considerable surprise that the pope should have done this, on his own authority, when the Council at his doorstep was engaged on precisely such problems. It is true that Catholic dogma asserts that, within the God-given limits of natural law and Revelation, the pope has absolute authority over the whole Church, independently of any Council, and John XXIII may have acted thus as a reminder of that fact.

In itself, no Catholic heart will feel any difficulty in accepting this. Looking at St Joseph in the perspective of scripture we can see him, in no way diminished in stature, as a man called to heroic faith in the fellowship of Abraham and the prophets. Devotion to St Joseph in the light of scripture can only be welcomed with joy. And yet it is a fact that in some countries and some congregations, devotion to St Joseph has taken a form which is part of an easily determined historical current. This is the current of nineteenth-century Catholicism. During that period countless congregations were created under the patronage of St Joseph, The Holy Family, the Child Jesus, Nazareth, etc. The human aspects of the Incarnation with its emotional overtones were the centre of interest. An iconography which is still very widespread followed this devotion; it would be interesting to study its origins, and the part played therein by ultramontanism, i.e. the Italian influence.

The mysteries of the childhood and humanity of Jesus are undeniably precious to the religious mind, and of unquestionable utility in the Christian life. The danger is, however, that they may come to take up all the room and thus to obscure the absolute primacy of the mystery of redemption, the paschal mystery: the death, burial, resurrection, ascension, and pentecost. An authentically biblical and Pauline point of view would concentrate upon Jerusalem. Bethlehem and Nazareth were only the preparation; they are presupposed. St Paul says that he does not want to know Christ 'according to the flesh'. In the flesh, born of a woman, born under the law (Gal. 4:4), Christ died. He rose again according to the Spirit, and it is this risen Christ who brings us to life and who is the origin of all salvation and holiness and life within the Alliance. If we pay undue attention to the human aspects of Jesus's life, and especially to those of his childhood, allowing his human development to become all-engrossing, we incur the risk of disturbing the equilibrium of the faith, stressing its tender and emotional aspects to the detriment of that vision which a true familiarity with the New Testament and particularly St Paul reveals to us.

Is it really possible to nourish our faith *simultaneously* with St Paul and with the 'Month of St Joseph'? Surely we must choose one *or* the other.[1]

Rome, 16 November, 1962

---

[1] See Document IV below, pp. 110-14

Chapter 9

The future of the Council

ON 12 NOVEMBER THE COUNCIL WAS INFORMED THAT its second session would be held from 12 May–29 June, 1963. Many were surprised at the lateness of this date which will coincide with the hottest season in Rome. A cardinal remarked: 'This is not going to be the second Vatican Council, but the second Council of Trent.' (Trent went on for practically twenty years.) Of course the Commissions will continue their work during the interval, and these will not be the preparatory Commissions nominated by the pope, but conciliar Commissions, two of which were elected by the Council, and which consist of prelates alone. But will the bishops want to be away from their dioceses for so long? Which experts will join the Commissions? Those who habitually live in Rome? Time will obviously be gained for conciliar discussions by careful preparation beforehand, but only if such preparation has been made in the spirit of the Council and along the lines it has laid down. Otherwise the scaffolding, erected with so much labour, will be demolished.

Two defects in the Council.

It cannot be denied that the Council is suffering from two defects: the absence of definite and reasonably limited standing orders, and the lack of some expeditious and more parliamentary way of getting through its work. That work has been prepared with due care in the preparatory pontifical Commissions in Rome, but not by the bishops. Much time would have been saved if the agenda, forwarded three or four months in advance, had been studied or discussed by local groups of bishops. If even now this suggestion is adopted there is still time to put it into effect before the second session.

The preparatory Commissions had worked out more than 70 Schemas, several of which duplicate each other— a result of not having combined Commissions and of that failure to co-ordinate work, which we have mentioned. A whole month was spent in examining a single one of these Schemas, and several sessions will be required for voting on the revised text. This month, however, has not been wasted; it has given time for the bishops to make contacts, to get to know each other, to take a general look at the Council's mechanism. But the danger of the Council being buried beneath a mass of paper and becoming a kind of 'Roman synod' claiming universal sanction remains very real. The synod of Rome in 1960 was regarded as a prelude to the Council; I personally hoped for much to come of it. The sum of its results was a pile of regulations and very little spiritual renewal. Many bishops consider that the Council should give priority to a limited number of really vital matters: that of the episcopate, implicit in many of the discussions; that of the ecumenical movement that so obviously corresponds to the will of God for the twentieth century; and whatever is directly concerned with the peace of the world and the dignity of the human person whose divine foundations are held in the Judaeo-Christian message.

A new reality in the Church: episcopal conferences.

From the point of view of internal affairs, the question of episcopal authority needs to be settled if the work of the past century, focused mainly on the authority of the papacy, is to be brought to a harmonious equilibrium. At the Council this problem has assumed a definite form: that of the status, function and authority of national episcopal conferences or of those that cover more extensive regions. As regards those conferences already existing (forty-two in number) it may be said that in the Council they have achieved self-awareness. This is true, with some qualifications and some perfectly understandable discrepancies, of all countries. Some groups are close-knit; the Dutch, for example, are among the best organized and most effective. The solidarity of other groups came as a surprise; a surprise, perhaps, to the groups themselves. We are thinking particularly of the Africans, whose unity is impressive. Including Madagascar, this group comprises 289 bishops, divided into two sections, one French speaking, the other English. Several times a single speaker voiced the unanimous decision of these 289 bishops. The South American group (nearly 600 bishops) is not so unified, but it is on the way to being so. It reveals a continent in the throes of renewal, springing especially from the theological centres of Chile and Buenos Aires. We are confronted, therefore, with the reality of an episcopate organized according to the natural divisions of mankind. This reality demands a status that is not merely administrative, but also canonical and theological. It is to be hoped that this will be bestowed by the Council. This would be a result of the greatest practicality, with the utmost promise for the future.

Will they come back?

Should this happen, it may be affirmed that, thanks to this Council the Church has entered a 'collegiate' stage in her pastoral government. Two or three years would not be excessive for a transition of such magnitude. It could not be rushed, and two years of conciliar life would mean that between two sessions the services of the Curia, so highly praised by Cardinal Ruffini, could be put at the disposal of other strictly episcopal bodies. Certainly two years would not be too long for such a change-over in the realm of theology, likewise, where many ideas have not yet attained the development or the maturity essential to them.

Unfortunately a number of bishops, and in particular those belonging to groups of such significance as the bishops of Africa and South America, have said that they will not come back for the second session. A strange decision; have they forgotten the oath to attend the Council which they took at their consecration? At the time, perhaps, they did not give it much thought, and now it may be a mere memory of the past. But the past has come to life in a rejuvenated present. They make money their excuse; the journey from South America costs a fortune.

Many bishops from impoverished countries have few priests and poor dioceses. But it would be impossible, unthinkable, that lack of money should prevent bishops from coming to the Council where their presence is so necessary. A minimal appeal to Christendom would bring in enough to pay for their journey ten times over. The Holy See is also ready to help, and it receives alms for the Council, some of them very humble. An old woman wrote to the pope: 'I had saved 10,000 francs. I know that the Council is expensive. I send them to you.'

The widow's mite.

This too is one of the aspects which make the Council evangelical. And perhaps it is one of those which count most in heaven.

16 November, 1962

Chapter 10

Outline of events,
14 November—26 November, 1962

14 *November*. During the 19th General Congregation Cardinal Ottaviani presented the five chapters of the theological Schema on the sources of Revelation: 1. The two sources of Revelation; 2. Inspiration and the literary forms used in Scripture; 3–4. The Old and New Testaments; 5. Holy Scripture in the Church.

This presentation was followed at once by criticisms of the Schema as a whole. The cardinals spoke first and set the tone in a general way for a discussion which was to exhibit two different tendencies.

16 *November*. In the 20th, 21st and 22nd general Congregations, a series of criticisms of the Schema as a whole.

20 *November*. At the 23rd general Congregation, under the presidency of Cardinal Frings, a vote was taken on the desirability of breaking off the study of the Schema. 1368 Fathers voted for the breaking off; 822 against. The voting was significant, but not decisive, since a two-thirds majority had not been attained.

21 *November*. Pope John XXIII informed the Council of his decision to adjourn the debate on the sources of

Revelation and to entrust a combined Commission of cardinals, members of the theological Commission and of the Secretariat for unity, with the task of producing a new version of the Schema.

25 *November*. Cardinal Cento introduces the Schema 'On the Means of Social Communication'[1] and Mgr Stourm (France) reads the report concerning it.

26 *November*. End of the discussion on modern means of communication, with the unanimous agreement of the assembly.

[1] See below, Document VI, p. 124.

Chapter 11

The Schema 'On the Sources of Revelation'

ON 14 NOVEMBER THE COUNCIL BEGAN TO EXAMINE the first dogmatic Schema, bearing the title: '*On the Sources of Revelation*'. This was clearly an unfortunate title because Revelation is *the* source, and what are called in this document 'sources of Revelation' i.e. scripture and tradition, are sources *only in relation to us*, only with reference to the way in which we become cognizant of what has been revealed. As regards Revelation itself, they are channels, ways or modes of transmission. The sixteenth-century Reformers made the mistake of separating them from and even of opposing them to each other, whereas the whole trend of traditional Catholic theology has been to unite them. Indeed not one of the Church's dogmas is based on either scripture or tradition *alone*. The two focus in unison like our two eyes which enable us to see the existence and the shape of things.

The press gave some idea of the criticisms and debates which the official Schema provoked. It has even described how the alternative formulae were proposed, although up to now (16 November) these have not been strained through the mesh of the theological Commission which alone is officially qualified to present such formulae to the assembly.

A 'Council of theologians'.

Within the ambit of the great Council, with its unity and universality, there exists, apart from the meetings between the bishops of the various countries and continents, a council of theologians. It has no mass meetings, no ceremonial, no banners. It is nonetheless real. More than a hundred, perhaps two hundred, theologians accompanied the bishops. Many of them are men actively engaged, sometimes with creative and dynamic effect, in the development of Catholic thought through the world, and particularly in Europe. They were not responsible for the documents of the preparatory Commissions which were officially submitted to the Fathers of the Council. In fact several of them were dismissed from these preparatory Commissions. To say that they are now having their revenge would be to discredit their character. It is natural that they should criticize documents whose teaching is so different and sometimes so remote from what they themselves think and say, as loyal Catholics and with scientific probity. This is why the official documents, at least that small part of them so far made public, have been subjected to a penetrating criticism, not lacking in force, without any attempt to please, even without mercy. The bishops want to be informed. Usually they have no time for intellectual activity. Here, they have; they have the means and the duty. They meet in groups, according to their languages or special interest, and together with theologians attend conferences or form groups. The long month spent on the liturgical Schema allowed time for this intellectual preparation, time to get to know and understand each other. It was an episcopate very much on the alert that approached the discussion of the first documents on dogma submitted to it.

16 *November: what will be the fate of the Schema.*

At the moment of writing, we do not know what the outcome will be; will the Schemas that have been presented be purely and simply discarded, 'buried' as unnecessary? Personally, we think that this would be a pity. It would indicate a development of that pragmatic attitude which we have noted above. Will they be amended by successive corrections? This is not intrinsically impossible or out of the question. But a document is not given a different character by altering a line here and there, or by changing some of its expressions. An apple tree always bears apples, and a cherry tree cherries. The same men will, ultimately, produce the same result and the fundamental style of the building will remain identical. In addition, such a procedure would consume weeks on end. In our opinion, it would be better to submit fresh documents to the assembly, prepared in the competent Commissions with the help of 'experts', representing the two opposing tendencies, neither exaggerating the differences nor minimizing their significance. This would not be difficult to achieve. As always, it depends entirely upon the men involved.

A new Commission for a new Schema.

At the end of a debate which lasted a week, the proposed contribution unhappily entitled 'On the two Sources of Revelation' has been sent back to be refashioned by a mixed Commission of cardinals and members of the theological Commission and of the Secretariat for unity (not all of whose members are bishops). This measure, asked for by a great number of bishops, was hailed with relief, like the relaxation and freshness that follows a long expected storm. This mixed commission has two presidents, Cardinal Ottaviani and Cardinal Bea, and thus has representatives of the two opposing tendencies at its head. It has been amusingly described as the 'Commission of the two sources'. Thus the frank admission of two tendencies has been given institutional status. What is really at stake?

Its immediate significance is that of a document intended for many years to dominate both Catholic teaching and theological research on the sources of our knowledge of what God has communicated to his People for the sustenance of their life. It is also a question of more generous or more restricted opportunities for Biblical study in the Church. Every Catholic holds that in the knowledge acquired through faith the two ways must be combined, somewhat in the way that our vision is the result of using both our eyes. Unfortunately, instead of speaking of two ways of communication, two means of reception, the Schema spoke of the two *sources of Revelation*. It thus failed to give the primacy to the unique and supreme source, the Word of God, foreshadowed in the Prophets, and delivered in its entirety to us in Jesus Christ; and not

in Christ's words alone, but in his life, his attitude to existence, his death; in short, in the sheer *fact* of Christ.

This issue: what is meant by doctrine?

A great number of the Fathers considered this omission
to be extremely grave, from the triple point of view of
evangelical truth, of the urgent pastoral need for sound
presentation of what the faith is and of the ecumenical
cause. It is certain that this presentation would have made
the dialogue with Protestants much more difficult. The
supporters of the official Schema have constantly maintained—and it was their sincere and profound conviction
—that the propounding of 'doctrine' is both the most important work of the pastoral ministry and the presupposi-
tion of all ecumenical activity that is to escape from a 'false
irenicism', i.e. a minimizing expression of the Catholic
faith. This conviction was likewise held by those who
wanted the Schema dismissed, and it is my own conviction
too. It would seem, therefore, that the difference arises in
the way in which doctrinal necessity and the very idea of
'doctrine' is understood.

The supporters of the Schema seem to hold that 'doctrine' consists of a certain number of affirmations that are
fixed and as it were deposited in standard formulae, presented to the mind like things or objects. These formulae
must at all costs be preserved, exhibited, and even brand-
ished like a statute of the Law. Those who are not satisfied
with the Schema believe that 'doctrine' cannot be divorced
from the activity of the mind that professes it; hence, together with the most thorough loyalty to this doctrine, they
include a constantly active *enquiry*. Whether what is in

question is its use in the pastoral ministry, or its ecumenical presentation, they consider its demands to be much more searching than could be met by stylistic readjustment or the avoidance of expressions psychologically wounding. From the pastoral point of view, this involves a vital re-thinking of doctrine and its development in such a way as to incorporate, with a view to answering them, the questions and the needs of the men to whom we are sent. From the ecumenical point of view, this means that we must take a fresh and profound look at the sources, and find the way to express their content with such integrity and fullness that the opposition that seems to exist on certain issues, but which is due to a restricted and perhaps superficial consideration, may be overcome. In the context of as complete, or even a deeper, loyalty to Catholic tradition, this would lead to a conception of doctrine and to an expression of it which our separated brethren could welcome and could accept as authentically related to what they, with us, hold to be the unquestionable principles of belief.

Repetitive teaching—or a faith that enquires.

If our interpretation is correct, the difference in attitude is that between teaching that is mere repetition and a faith that is active and enquiring. The point deserves closer attention, and to this end various studies undertaken during this century would prove helpful, especially a little known work by Maurice Blondel, published not only under a pseudonym, but with a curious title, *La Semaine Sociale de Bordeaux et le Monophorisme*, in 1910.

The discussions—they might even be called the conflict

—over the Schema on the two sources illustrated also two points of decisive importance for understanding conciliary procedure, and, more generally, the way of life in the Catholic Church: 1. The co-existence of disagreement with a fundamental agreement on basic matters. 2. The way in which, in the Church, the divine element is associated with the human and acts through it.

Disagreement is compatible with the most genuine communion in belief.

St Augustine made his own a striking remark of St Cyprian: *'Licet, salvo jure communionis, diversum sentire'*: different ways of thinking are permissible so long as communion (in the faith) is observed. The Fathers of the Council, divided by certain intellectual convictions, have taken part in the same Eucharist and have said together the prayer *Adsumus*. They have not merely displayed good manners in discussion and shown that charity towards individuals which prevents any aspersions on their good will, but all have expressed a common and absolute respect for those factors which are normative for every Catholic: Holy Scripture, the tradition of the Fathers of the Church, the solemn decisions of the Councils and the magisterium and, in particular, those of the Council of Trent and of the first Vatican Council. In fact it was the admirable decree of Trent that was invoked by many who criticized the Schema; which, they said, in contrast with Trent did not establish as the absolutely primary source the Gospel, promised by the Prophets, wholly fulfilled by Christ the Son of God, and entrusted by him to his Apostles that they might spread it abroad. A journalist could not be

decried for presenting all this theatrically, as an open conflict between definite individuals. And yet some press ac-
counts, although factually correct, are in danger of missing
the real spirit of the Council, which is one of trust and
mutual respect ... it is neither a fairy-tale nor a nest of
vipers, but the confrontation of men deeply united in the
communion of the same faith.

*In the Church the divine and human elements inter-
mingle.*

For us, historians and theologians, it was a moving event.
We have been privileged to live through an experience of
the kind we have so often studied in the earlier Councils:
Ephesus, Trent, Vatican I. We have seen how God leads
his Church into truth and makes use of the extremely
human initiatives of men. When two sides confront each
other, as in the present issue, there are not only formal
speeches; during the session the unexpected turns up, as
it will do when a discussion is in earnest; groups meet;
papers are read; ideas crop up; when a vote is necessary
a document will be drawn up with this in mind; in short,
the human element is present in all such procedures. The
final result will be what God wants. Each man plays his
part, but God who takes part in the action joins in with
the human players. For he is transcendant enough, supreme enough, to achieve what he wants through the activity
of human freedom acting on its own.

The theological term for God's way of acting thus is
'assistance'. This is distinct from 'inspiration'. Even when
he 'inspired' the Prophets or St Paul, for example, God
moved the mind and will of his messengers without doing

violence to them, illuminating them from within. But this was a positive intervention, something from beyond themselves; he *added* something not contributed by man. But, with 'assistance', he leaves men to their own resources; they have to seek and find for themselves. His part in the affair is simply that of so conducting matters that what *men* have found, deliberated on and expressed, shall have *his* guarantee, which is that of absolute Truth. The work of the Council belongs to this aspect of Providence. It is entirely human, but God is not absent from it. His Spirit, as on the first day of creation, hovers over the troubled waters, and he ensures that they will be calmed and reach truth in the end.

Rome, 2 December

Chapter 12

Ecumenical overture: the observers
are satisfied

THE PRESENCE OF THIRTY-SEVEN OBSERVERS FROM
non-Roman Catholic Christian communions is one of
the major elements in the sequence of events leading up
to the council.[1] They have been seated in a gallery close to
the Presidency, almost opposite the cardinals. The usual
question asked about them is desperately banal: are they
happy? Their own frank answer is: yes. The welcome
and, better still, the trust shown to them has done more
than volumes of apologetic to remove those feelings of mis-
trust which are often more powerful than rational objections, and in any case lend insurmountable weight to such
objections. They have been present at a debate which they
could see would pave the way for that future dialogue of
which their presence is as it were the harbinger. One of
them remarked that this was the first time that the Catholic Church had washed its dirty linen in public. The
wind of change that this implies clears the air for a closer
rapport in the future. Nevertheless we should not yield
to a facile optimism. We are merely at the foot, under

[1] See list of Observers, Document VII, p. 129.

improved conditions, of the approach to those grave disagreements which divide us. It will take generations for the miraculously sown seed to ripen. The ecumenical dialogue is just beginning.

Yes, miraculously sown. There is something miraculous in the French community of Protestant monks at Taizé. There is something miraculous in Cardinal Bea's Secretariat for Christian Unity. The participation of the observers in the Council is miraculous. Miraculous too, is the fact—and it is a fact—that all, or to make allowance for the unknown, almost all the Fathers of the Council have affirmed their adherence to an ecumenical purpose. An impressive number, from every country, formally declared this with a sincerity which was obvious and, to us, very moving. We thank God for it.

The ecumenical spirit at the council is not homogenous.

And yet all do not seem to be at the same stage, not all share the same authentic ecumenical outlook. In fact three levels, differing in depth and authenticity, may be distinguished; the third presupposes and incorporates the second, as the second does the first.

The first level does not amount to more than a sincere feeling of goodwill shown by a desire to avoid what would cause needless pain to 'the others'. 'Doctrine' is accepted and expounded in its classical or even its scholastic formulations without any attempt to arrive at its deeper understanding, trying merely to express it with greater clarity and to compensate for its resultant rigidity by a courteous and charitable attitude. This is good, but does not go far enough.

At the second level there is an appreciation of the possibilities and difficulties of those 'others', a concern to understand the obstacles they encounter through the image they have formed of what we hold, and a response to their real difficulties by making an effort towards adaptation. This is better, but still does not go far enough.

We must, in fact, go further, and welcome with the same intensity as we hold the Catholic truth the salutary impact that dialogue with non-Catholics is bound to have; and we must enrich our own doctrinal ideas through steeping them in the deepest sources of Biblical Revelation and authentic Catholic tradition. This is not to take the road to liberalism; far from it; it is not a minimal approach; it is the way to a maximal doctrinal expression, the way to a conversion that is both spiritual and intellectual. A spiritual conversion because it involves a radical criticism of our own attitudes of possessiveness, self-righteousness, self-justification, our spirit of argumentative or denominational triumph. An intellectual conversion, for we must strive to move beyond the comfortable and settled possession of a truth that involves no problems, and attain an idea of doctrine that is equally traditional, but broader and able to integrate those aspects of truth which the questions of our separated brethren compel us to treat more seriously. When we embark on this we realize that the road ahead is still a long one, and that we have barely started on it. It is a work of generations, demanding fidelity, patience, prayer and hope.

Rome, 2 December

Chapter 13

Outline of events, 26 November—5 December, 1962

26 *November*: At the end of the 27th general congregation presided over by Cardinal Tisserant, the 2133 Fathers present began the study of the Schema prepared by the Commission for the eastern Churches on Unity.

27–28–30 *November*: The discussion on the Schema was continued in the general congregations, which also made some examination of modern means of communication and the liturgy.

1 *December*: The Fathers accepted Mgr Felici's proposal and voted on the following text: 'The examination of the decree on the Unity of the Church having been completed, the Fathers of the Council give it their approval as a document which contains the accepted truths of faith, and as a sign of their interest and good will towards the separated brethren of the East. But, in conformity with the observations and statements put forward in the hall of the Council, this decree shall form a single document with the decree on ecumenism and the chapter on the same subject contained in the Schema on the dogmatic constitution of the Church.' 2068 votes were given in favour of its adoption; 36 against.

1 *December*: The Schema on the Church was introduced by Cardinal Ottaviani and presented by Mgr Franic (Yugoslavia).

3–4–5 *December*: Various criticisms of the Schema on the Church.

Chapter 14

The Council discusses Christian unity and the Church

THE METHOD OF PROCEDURE LAID DOWN FOR VATICAN II is conducive to the criticism of the documents presented to it. At the First Vatican Council the member who presented a document did not merely hand over a document prepared by a pre-conciliary Commission and leave it at that: he explained and defended it, answered criticisms and discussed the suggested amendments. There were discussions not merely about the text but between the upholders of different points of view. At Vatican II the text put forward may be attacked and criticised, or even applauded—approval has not been lacking—but it will not be, in the technical sense, defended. When arguments pro and contra have been expressed, it is sent back, without being really discussed across a table, to the conciliar Commission for an examination of these points. If it has received, as a whole and in its various parts, more approval than criticism—in the case of the Liturgy this was almost triumphantly so—then all the Commission has to do is to produce a corrected version of the text. This is a very detailed and concentrated task; how detailed may be

gathered from the fact that for the first two chapters of
the Schema on the Liturgy alone, the Commission had to
cope with 2000 suggestions. The Fathers have been impressed by the earnest way in which the Commission does
its work and by the obvious care taken when an amendment is either adopted or rejected. When the preface and
the first chapter came back from the workshop of the Commission they were welcomed by what amounted to virtual
unanimity.

After a somewhat hasty survey of the long-winded
Schema: 'On the means of communication between men',
which will be committed to a pastoral Directory, the
Council began in its two concluding weeks to discuss an
important document on Christian unity, *Ut omnes unum
.int,* and the main section of the Schema on the constitution of the Church.

The preliminary format of the Decree on Unity.

The preliminary format of the Decree on Christian
Unity contains a number of good things. But it suffers
from the same defect as all the preliminary preparations
for the Council: lack of co-operation between the different
working groups, the absence of an overall and directing
vision. The text, which was composed by the Commission
for the Eastern Churches, did not take into account the
total ecumenical picture, did not include in its perspective
the World Council of Churches to which practically all
the Orthodox Churches belong. It sprang from a pre-
ecumenical eirenicism, which was so notably promoted by
Leo XIII and Pius XI. It therefore needs to be brought
up-to-date with the present stage of ecumenical enquiry,

with which two other documents are cognizant; one, already submitted to the Council, is a chapter from the Schema on the Church; the other, not yet published, is to come from the Secretariat for Unity. The Council has decided that the three documents shall be considered together, and that the one on the Eastern Churches shall be given that special consideration which their close doctrinial relationship with us deserves.

The members of the Secretariat for Unity are much in demand.

So a vast amount of work remains to be done. Once again, many of the Fathers, a majority perhaps, believe that a solution is to be found in a combined Commission, drawn from three Commissions; that for Theology, for the Eastern Churches, and the Secretariat for Unity. This was the solution adopted for the Schema on the so-called 'Sources of Revelation'. The same refuge has been sought for the *Ut omnes unum sint*. This is becoming a habit. It is a somewhat naïve solution: the members of the Secretariat are not numerous enough to reshape the whole project, nor are they necessarily the most competent to do so. But the fact that they were sought out is significant, and the reason seems obvious. The Secretariat is the one institution that has been officially established for the purpose of dialogue. The Fathers turn to it in order to secure the frank discussion they desire. Two or three significant votes have indicated that a good two-thirds majority are anxious for such discussion. If there were opportunities in, for example, the Commission on the pastoral ministry or if a Secretariat for urgent world problems existed—an institution demanded by many—there is no doubt that they would be as eagerly sought out.

Everything must be considered in terms of a mission to the whole world.

There is one Commission which, in our opinion, should enter into the discussion—the Commission for Missions; that is, unless we consider this merely as a body of technicians rather than as an instrument devised to serve the Church's expansion, or for the spread of the gospel through the Church. It is surprising that missionary affairs have been so little to the fore during this session. Of course, missionary concern does exist and is very much in the context of that anxiety for the pastoral ministry so constantly expressed by the Fathers; and yet it is also rather swamped by the general nature of that context.

Much as we welcome the recent changeover from 'missions' to 'Mission of the Church', from the idea of a church already established and at rest, on the one hand and, on the other—as some kind of adjunct—a church involved in expeditions to foreign parts, to the idea that there is only one Church, that is a whole, always and everywhere evangelical—yet do we feel that a good deal is lost by not having in the forefront of our minds the *specific* problems of the Mission of the Church in regions other than the western world, which is at home with classical theology. These regions urgently call for generosity and a spirit of enterprise. Have we forgotten the inspiration that made Francis Xavier believe that he could convert the Indies and China and Japan? From a different point of view, these regions have a great deal to give us. Their problems are relevant to ours; the way they deal with their problems can supplement the way we have hitherto tackled our own. This is essential, it is the challenge this middle third of a remarkably creative century offers us. We learn to decline verbs in the first, second and third person singular or plural; so we should accustom ourselves to declining the problems of the Church, the Liturgy, unity, in terms of Africa, America, Asia, the world. Two-thirds of the world's population live in Asia. It follows that we must rethink everything in terms of a mission and of a mission that is world-wide. A Schema on unity, a Schema on the Church, developed from this angle, would, whilst holding to eternal truths, satisfy our minds in a new way. The Church would be ahead of the world, for this is an attitude that the world itself will come to adopt. Precisely because we have gone beyond the concept of missions to THE Mission, and because today we recognize better that Mission is as it were an inherent dimension of the Church, coextensive with it, therefore this idea of Mission has a contribution to make to every single problem that faces the Church.

In the century of the Church.

In 1922 Romano Guardini wrote: 'A religious event of immense significance is about to occur: the Church is regaining a place in the human mind.' In 1926 O. Dibelius published a book entitled *The century of the Church*. The twentieth century has been the century of much else besides: the ecumenical movement, the atom, the liberation of the colonies, psycho-analysis, the conquest of space, communism. . . . But together with all this, it is also, without any doubt, the century of the Church, or of a new understanding of the Church. This is the reason why it was hoped that the Schema *De Ecclesia,* on the constitution of the Church, would incorporate and present in a balanced synthesis the results of forty years' study of ecclesiological problems. All the Fathers agreed that to some extent this had been achieved; but if left much to be desired. The Fathers also wanted an exposition of the Church as a whole which they could offer to modern men, whereas the preparatory Commission had only concerned itself with certain aspects of doctrine specifically related to present needs. Finally, the Fathers wanted Vatican II to be a real completion of Vatican I. The latter only managed to finish one chapter of its constitution of the Church, that which dealt with the visible head of the Church militant and with the papal prerogatives. The intention of Vatican II is to balance this account by developing the chapter on the episcopate; its function, its nature, its authority within the body of the Church.

The majority of the Fathers, whilst approving the work so far done and submitted to them, wanted it to be taken further and developed both into a doctrinal synthesis and as a clarification of the function of bishops, with special reference to what is implied in the consecration of bishops and to the nature of their 'collegiate' function. In practice this means that the Schema itself required refurbishing and revising. From the remarks of a number of Fathers it seems obvious that, failing a thorough revision, the Schema will suffer the same fate as that on the 'Sources of Revelation' and be thrown out in the second session— yet it is meant to be the main feature of that session.

Chapter 15

Outline of events,
5 December—8 December, 1962

5 *December*: At the 34th general Congregation, with Cardinal Alfrink as President, 2114 Fathers being present, the members of the Council were given a document containing a list of the various subjects that form the programme of Vatican II. The number of Schemas has been reduced from the 73 named by the central Commission to 20.

6 *December*: Mgr Felici informs the Council of John XXIII's decree on the work to be done between the sessions.

7 *December*: The pope's speech at the end of the first session.[1]

8 *December*: Solemn closure of the first session.

[1] See Document V, pp. 115-23.

Chapter 16

Looking towards the second session

THE OPENING DATE OF THE SECOND SESSION HAS BEEN transferred from 12 May to 8 September, 1963. This session should last for at least three months and will consider, if not settle, the main problems with which the council has to deal. It is a pity that so far the Council has worked without a definite programme and without previously established standing orders. This has led to a certain lack of sense of direction. But much was learnt in the first session from experience, from the search for a common outlook and method, and from the discovery of contemporary trends and deep-rooted hopes. . . .

Nine months will divide the second session from the first. Something is coming to birth, but what? When the Fathers parted for this long interval, the idea was that good use should be made of the period between the two sessions. There was work to be done in two places: in Rome by the Commissions—not the preparatory Commissions nominated by the pope, but those chosen by the Council and the pope in the circumstances described above; and in the countries to which the bishops had returned, this time with the intention of making a collective study of the conciliar documents already received, or of revising them.

In Rome the Commissions should uphold the spirit of the Council and bear in mind the directives given by the great majority of the Fathers. These have been formulated during two months of personal meetings and discussions and are on the whole sufficiently precise.

In the various countries of the world it is to be hoped that now the preparatory work which was not done before the first session will be done. The success of the second session will largely depend on this. Certainly the Council had been carefully prepared in the Roman Commissions. But apart from the fact that these worked in isolation from each other, they also developed their working papers in a spirit very different from that which prevailed at the Council. The criticism which ensued revealed how great that difference was. The Council, i.e. the bishops, or rather the various episcopates, ought also to have been prepared. For this to be possible, the bishops should have received the documents well in advance. This would have made possible: 1. A collective study of them by bishops assembled in conference, or at least by representative Commissions, with experts to help them. 2. Written criticisms or counter-proposals that could have been considered before a provisionally definitive text was submitted to the Council. Without such preliminary consideration, the work has to be done, somewhat hastily, in the Council itself. But what failed to be achieved before the first session may well be accomplished before the second. Everything points that way.

A shadow falls on this cheerful prospect: the pope's

health. At the end of the first session, many were worried about the man whom all regarded with affectionate respect. May God preserve for us the man who has gathered us around him in the greatest assembly of all time. And if God decides to take him from us, may Elijah be replaced by Elisha, inheriting not only his mantle and responsibility, but also his spirit! [1]

---

[1] Since this was written, of course, John XXIII has been followed by Paul VI, who has pronounced himself ready to further the ends to which John XXIII gave himself.

Chapter 17

The laity at the Council[1]

THERE IS NO DOUBT THAT THE LAITY DO HAVE A PART in the Council. We shall try to explain how this is so. Does it spring solely from their interest, from their prayer —and many are praying very intensely—through which they co-operate with God's work, as the community in Jerusalem did when Peter was imprisoned? What further part do they play? This is what we shall try to find out, with regard to the first session that has just ended; the second, due to begin on 8 September; and the long intermediary period that separates and yet links the two.

The 'moral' presence of the laity.

The laity have been physically present at the Council only in the person of the Protestant observers, the workmen in the aisles (e.g. firemen) and a friendly scholar or so, given a place among the observers. Morally they have been present in a real and profound sense (not like Topaz, who received his academic laurels 'morally speaking'). We have not tired of saying how during the preparatory

[1] This chapter first appeared as an article in *'Témoignage Chrétien'* 21.12.1962.

period of the Council, although the laity had no direct part in its labours, what they thought and desired was felt to a greater degree that might be imagined. The bishops are aware of their thoughts and desires and, on the whole, champion them and keep them in mind. One is reminded of a photographic print which reveals what is hidden in the negative, or how, at the Planetarium, a whole world we do not normally see becomes apparent when the lights are dimmed. If only there were a spiritual camera that would reveal the thought and feelings of the heart. . . . Such a camera would have shown that existing in the bishops' minds and hearts were the people entrusted to them; in the first place Christians but, as well, all men, whether relatively sympathetic or quite alien. . . .

We had a glimpse of this in the pastoral bias which was affirmed at every opportunity and even demanded for the dogmatic constitutions: so much so that one might ask whether the requirements of precision and austerity, proper to such documents, might not be lost sight of. A further sign is to be found in the tardy and cautious but very moving appeal made by Cardinal Lercaro in particular for a 'Church of the Poor' and for priority to be given to the great issues at stake in the world today: peace, hunger, the dignity of man and the respect due to it, racial equality. These questions which are in the minds of the bishops of all countries will probably be considered during the second session and lead to decisions, some of which have already been foreshadowed.

The Church exists for men.

It must be realized, however, that although none of

these great human needs can be alien from the Council, the council is not a Catholic version of Bandung or the United Nations. Necessary as it is for the world-wide gathering of bishops to express the mind of the gospel and proclaim its ruling on the problems raised by a stricken world, it is not for this reason that they have come together at the tomb of the Apostle Peter. The truth is that the Council in its own way is experiencing and living through that tension which the whole Church is experiencing, and which may be summarized thus: the Church exists in itself, but it does not exist *for itself;* it exists for men, for men to be led to Jesus Christ. In this way the Church exists both *in itself* and *in the world*. In the basic examination of conscience begun at the Council, and which is perhaps more thorough than one had dared hope or at least expect, it is discovering problems both *ad intra* and *ad extra,* problems relating to its own intrinsic character and to its relationship with man.

Its problems *ad intra* are those, for example, of the Liturgy, of the status and function of the episcopate, of the adaptation of Canon Law to modern needs. They concern the Church herself and are often primarily clerical matters. But even in this case their purpose is to serve men so that they may be led to Christ, and are thus bound up with the Church's mission, inseparable from her nature. It follows that, in spite of inevitable appearances of self-regard and concern with solely clerical matters, at no moment does the Church forget either the laity or the world. We might even apply here what Péguy says about children in the life of adults: 'Everything we do, we do on their account. Nothing is done except for their sakes!'

A brief forecast.

We are now at a stage from which some forecast can be made about the second session and the work to be done in the interim. We now know the principle on which the conciliary Commissions work. We may also hazard a guess as to the way in which the second session will open. Cardinal Suenens and Cardinal Montini have made statements with regard to this which not only correspond to the hopes expressed by a great number of the Fathers, but also seem to have been given papal approval.

The Council, they have said, has far too much unrelated material to deal with. Its work must be limited and organized. It must be related to the two poles of the Church *ad intra* and the Church *ad extra,* and to their respective needs. This involves, first, a sound presentation of the inner reality of the Church and a clearer account of her apostolic constitution (the episcopate) and, secondly, the elucidation of what is needed for her mission and for witness to the gospel at the service of men in the modern world.

A problem of this kind is of direct concern to the laity, for it includes their part both in the evangelization of the world and in the Church's inner life. The Liturgy concerns them; the Schema dealing with it took up the whole of the month of October and was entirely concerned to find ways and means by which the people might take a fuller part in the liturgical action. The constitution of the Church concerns them, even in those aspects, such as the authority and status of the episcopate, which seem most purely technical, because their clarification is required for an improvement in the Church's liturgical, pastoral and missionary adaptation in the different regions of the world. And in that divine constitution, *the laity have their own position.*

From this point of view we are unable to agree with a proposition, which was put forward by one of the Fathers of the Council with the aim, laudable in itself, of avoiding duplication in conciliar documents. Since there exists an ample Schema prepared by the Commission on the laity dealing with the status and activities of the laity in the Church, this Father proposed that chapter 6 of the dogmatic Schema on the Church, dealing with the laity, should be withdrawn and its content transferred to the more immediately pastoral document prepared by the Commission on the laity. It may indeed be possible to abridge this 6th chapter of the dogmatic Constitution but, in our view, it is most important and even essential for its susbstance to be retained in the dogmatic Constitution on the Church and that the theological foundation of all pastoral work carried out by the laity, all active participation of the people in the Liturgy, should be affirmed in conjunction with the chapters on the nature and the mission of the Church, on the episcopate and papal primacy, in the setting of a strictly theological doctrine of the Church. In this statement, those glorious phrases that have come to life again in the last thirty years, and have been so aptly included in the Schema—phrases that depict the priestly, regal and prophetic character of the People of God —must be retained. Without them the resulting image of the Church would be clerical, incomplete and unbalanced.

The laity at the second session of the Council.

Thus the laity will be present at the second session by virtue of the matters that will be dealt with there. Will they be present in any other way? Will lay 'experts' be summoned to the Council and their services used during the intermediary period? Up to the present their testimony has been heard only indirectly, or even from far off, in the preparatory stages of the Council.[1] Nothing intrinsically rejects such a direct summons any more than it rejects direct participation in the preparatory period. Yet the laity were hardly given a direct hearing during the preparatory period. The Schemas were prepared with the greatest care, and yet it is fair to ask whether some of their defects might not have been avoided had they been prepared with the collaboration of the laity. The Fathers of the Council, who know the documents and are aware of the criticisms they have provoked, are in a position to answer this question. As regards the eventual summoning of expert laymen, it may be that the directives given on 5 December by Cardinal Cicognani, the Secretary of State, with the pope's approval, may provide a pointer in this direction. These are his words:

'Consultations and questioning may also be profitably undertaken with regard to those who, not from their official position, but from reasons of respect and sound method (*humanitas*) are held to be experienced in different

---

[1] Since these lines were written: (a). A score or so of genuinely representative people have been consulted (in April, 1963) on the problems to be dealt with by Schema XVII. (b). It has been announced that lay members of the large international catholic organizations may be present as consultants at the Council. (c). It is rumoured that even women, and also nuns, may be consulted.

spheres of activity, especially in the external works of the apostolate. . . .'

Does this refer to members, especially heads of departments, of the Curia, who are connected in some way with the subject matter of a given conciliary Commission? This may well be so and would be understandable. Still the passage is couched in the most general terms, and does not in itself set any limit to the consultations suggested or to courteous exchange of information.

In any case, the opinion of the Catholic people, intelligently informed about conciliar matters by the Catholic press, has played a great part in the formation of a Catholic mind which, through the assembled bishops, has produced that remarkable and tonic 'spirit of the Council' which we hope may continue to blow healthily throughout the coming year. This opinion must continue to be well informed and to express itself freely, without impatience or uproar, without reserve or faintheartedness. The Council will profit from this in its second and decisive session, and in its turn the world also will benefit from the work of a Council thus circumstanced and upheld.

With an obvious backward glance at Jansenism Pascal said: 'When we have a good pope, may he find the Church still in uproar.' When the second session of the Council opens may it find the Church still big with desire.

Rome, 9 December

Chapter 18

What we have learnt from the first session, and what we may hope for in the future

IT IS GENERALLY AGREED THAT THIS FIRST SESSION has suffered from the lack of a programme, from lack of direction. Its aims have been too vast. In the preparatory work absence of unity has been manifested in a plethora of documents. During the last general Congregations a balance-sheet was drafted, and some attempt at forecasting development was made.

This balance-sheet is in many respects positive; we shall return to it. Even so, it is obvious that the Council cannot cope with all the material prepared for it. There was talk of seventy-three Schemas: these have been reduced to twenty. Even with twenty, the Council will be forced to concentrate and impose some unity on all the various theses, and leave a huge amount of practical and technical labour to the Commissions, simply giving them general directives. It has been suggested—and the idea seems to reflect the pope's intentions—that the second session should focus its work on the Church considered first in herself and then in her relationship with mankind.

The Church herself; that is, a synthesizing view of the various aspects of her nature, which will include her mission to the world and the clarification of the doctrine of the episcopate which we discussed above. The Church in her relationship with mankind; this implies making a statement and reaching decisions with regard to the main human issues; peace and armaments; hunger and poverty; the dignity of the human person and racial equality. It also means that the missionary idea must be increasingly incorporated as a dynamic factor in the whole of the Church's activity.

The work goes on.

In order to channel in this direction the work which is to form the immediate preparation for the second session certain rules were specified, with the pope's approval, on 5 December. Quoting the most decisive passage of his speech on 11 October,[1] they stress that the work as a whole must be adapted to the *purpose of the Council,* not to refurbish nor even to provide theses of classical theology, but to express both as regards their form and content the vital points of the deposit of faith in a way that will fill the requirements of a teaching authority intent on its pastoral ministry, i.e. in a way that will meet the human problems of our time.

In order to make sure that the work of the intermediary period does take this line and that the conciliary Commissions do effectively work in co-operation with each other and *in the spirit of the Council,* which is now plain enough,

[1] Document II, pp. 97-105.

a special Commission has been created for continuation and co-ordination.

Bernanos wrote: 'It is all very well to have programmes for social reform on paper. But what matters is the men you will call upon to put them into practice' (*Nous autres Français*, 1939, p. 241). To set up a Commission is admirable. The important thing, however, is *who* will be its members. We have heard today that these are to be Cardinals Liénart, Suenens, Spellman, Doepfner, Confalonieri, Urbani, from the general Secretariat, Mgr Felici, and five under-secretaries, including Mgr Villot, coadjutor bishop of Lyons. These are men of decision and provide a guarantee that the spirit of the Council will be maintained throughout the work that has to be carried on until September.

A provisional balance-sheet.

A balance-sheet of work done has been issued: in less than two months more than 500 Fathers have spoken, more than 500 others have put forward amendments in writing. Four Schemas have been examined. The beginning of the Schema on the Liturgy, which involves the principles and spirit of the entire Schema, was put to the vote after most carefully considered amendments. . . .

But the real balance-sheet of the Council lies elsewhere. This must be said in order to answer the understandable impatience of those who ask: 'What decisions have in fact been taken?'—to say nothing of those whose passionate hostility makes understanding impossible—like a woman member of some sect who wrote to me and among many other pettinesses remarked: 'The seven hills have brought forth a mouse!'

Briefly and clearly, what can be put on the credit side of this first session? This should be looked for not primarily in the domain of what has been decided, but in that of a psychological and moral fact, an experience and a spirit. Personally we find it impossible to doubt that even if the council had not decided anything and were not to decide anything, even if this first session could not be succeeded by another, one fact of incalculable significance has already emerged. Something irrevocable has been produced and affirmed in the Church.

The episcopate has discovered itself. It has seen itself. It has become aware of itself. Out of this awareness, the formulae will come. They will turn up of their own accord, provided the door is left open. We have already described that strongly felt experience which we shared with so many others—the unique and incontrovertible evidence of the simple fact of the Council's existence. Through it each of those taking part becomes in many respects a different man. Tendencies that had lain dormant in him come to life; whilst others that had been uppermost discreetly withdraw. He feels uplifted by the realization of what he has in common with men of other races and different outlook. And he reaches complete awareness of the solidarity and the world-wide responsibility of the episcopate. The humdrum image of a bishop in his palace, alone at the head of a diocese whose ordinary business has something trivial about it, vanishes into thin air. Each bishop feels that he is a member of a body that knows no limit in space or time: the body of the apostolic Pastorate of which Jesus Christ is the invisible head (cf. 1 Peter, 5:4), and whose universal pastorate is visibly reflected in that of Peter's successor.

The spirit of the Council.

The animating spirit of this great body is now apparent. Not that it is wholly shared by everyone of the bishops or held with complete unanimity. We have neither concealed nor exaggerated the tensions that have made themselves felt. But whatever may be true of given individuals, the Council does have a spirit which has come into being and found expression and which is very much one with that of Pope John XXIII. It is a spirit of frankness and freedom, free from all servility and self-seeking intrigue; it is at the service of mankind, seeking neither power nor privilege; it is evangelical and apostolic, a spirit of reverence and love for men, anxious to honour their freedom and dignity; it is open-minded towards others and has dropped any suggestion of scoring theological or clerical points. Lastly, it is a sustained attentiveness to hear what God, who does speak through events, is asking from his Church today. The observers have been impressed by the serious examination of conscience which the Church, in the person of her pastors, has embarked upon, so that she may serve her Lord more worthily.

We are not awarding laurels or distributing prizes, but outlining a programme drawn up by the Council itself, which received it from the Spirit who assembled it and who will reassemble it in the future. *Dominus qui incepti ipse perficiat!* May the Lord who began this great work, himself ensure its completion.

Strasbourg, 18 December 1962

Documents

Document I

Adsumus

THE PRAYER ADSUMUS WAS SAID BEFORE EACH MEET-
ing of the Central Commission during the work of preparation for the Council and before each session of the
Council. It was probably composed by St Isidore of Seville
(619) and was used at the Council of Toledo (633).

We come before thee, O Lord Holy-Spirit, still burdened by the weight of our sins, but nevertheless assembled
in thy name.

Come to us. Be with us. Mercifully enter our hearts.
Teach us what we should do. Show us the path we should
take. Effect what it is our duty to perform.

Be the sole source of our inspiration, and the sole author
of our decisions, Thou who alone with God the Father and
his Son dost possess the glorious name.

Keep us from offending against righteousness, Thou
who dost supremely love what is right. May ignorance not
lead us to evil. May success not sway us. May we not be
corrupted by bribes or by human respect.

But really join us to thyself, through the gift of thy
grace alone, so that we may be one in thee, and never in
any way stray from the truth.

Gathered together therefore, in thy name, keeping to what is right in all things, guided by compassion, may we reach our decisions without in any way departing from thee and may our deeds, having been well done, earn for us an everlasting reward.   Amen.

Document II

The opening speech of John XXIII at the Second Vatican Council

The following passage gives the essential parts of the speech made by John XXIII on 11 October, 1962, to the Fathers, the non-Catholic observers, the official delegations and the notabilities assembled in the basilica of St Peter for the opening of Vatican II.

IT IS OUR STRONG HOPE THAT THE CHURCH, ENLIGHT-ened by this Council, will augment her spiritual resources, acquire renewed energy and be able to face the future without fear. Granted the necessary adaptations and a proper mutual collaboration, the Church will act so that men, families and nations may turn their minds to heavenly things.

This is why the celebration of the Council makes us proclaim, in gratitude to the giver of all gifts, full of joy, the glory of Christ our Lord, glorious and immortal King of all ages and all nations.

Towards a new order in human relations.

There is a further consideration, Venerable Brethren, which it is useful to tell you. Indeed, in order that the cup of our holy joy may be full, we want to give this great assembly the encouraging account of circumstances of great promise in which this ecumenical Council is beginning.

During the customary exercise of our pastoral ministry certain suggestions came to our ears from men who though of unquestioned zeal lacked breadth of vision, discretion and a sense of proportion.

These persons see in the modern age only destructiveness and the perversion of truth: our time, they say, in comparison with the past, is essentially degenerate; they behave as though they have learnt nothing from history, which is, nevertheless, the shaping force of life, and as though in the days of the earlier ecumenical Councils, Christian thought and life and due religious freedom enjoyed an undisputed triumph.

It really does seem necessary for us to express our disagreement with these prophets of woe, forever predicting catastrophes as if the end of the world were at hand.

In the present state of affairs Providence is leading us to a new order of human relationships. It is using the work of man, often in a way different from man's expectations, to bring about its supreme and unexpected objectives and everything, including human differences, is working for the greater good of the Church.

The truth of this is easy to see if we look carefully at the modern world. That world is busy with political and economic affairs, and no longer has the time to concern itself with those spiritual problems with which the magisterium of holy Church has to deal. Of course this is not a right attitude and it must be reproved. At the same time, it cannot be denied that the new conditions of modern life have removed countless obstacles by which the children of the world formerly hindered the free activity of the Church. The merest glance at the Church's history is sufficient to reveal how even the ecumenical Councils, a series of glorious events in the life of the Catholic Church, often experienced grave difficulties and much distress during their celebration, as a result of undue interference from the civil power. The princes of this world sometimes offered their services as faithful defenders of the Church, but this was not without loss and spiritual danger, for they performed this service from self-interested and dangerous political motives.

In this connection, we are moved to express our grief at the fact that a great number of bishops, most dear to us, are compelled to be absent from us; they are either in prison for their loyalty to Christ or restrained by other impediments. Their memory stirs us to offer our fervent prayer to God for them.

Nevertheless, it is with great hope and encouragement that today we see that the Church, finally delivered from those numerous obstacles of a secular nature which she was wont to encounter in the past, through you is now enabled to make her majestic and sonorous voice heard from this Vatican basilica as if from a new Upper Room.

The modern defence and manifestation of the truth.

The Council's chief objective is this: that the sacred deposit of Christian doctrine shall be maintained and taught in a more effective form. Such a doctrine necessarily embraces the whole man, soul and body, and because men are pilgrims on this earth it directs their journey to heaven.

This means that we must regulate our mortal life so that we can perform our duties as citizens of both earth and heaven, and thus reach the goal set by God. It means that all men, individually or as a social group, must unswervingly aim throughout life at the possession of heavenly goods, use earthly goods for that purpose alone, and never permit their use to become a threat to eternal happiness.

The Lord said: 'Make it your first care to find the kingdom of God and his approval' (Matt. 6:33). The word *first* shows where our mind and energy should be directed. Nevertheless the words that follow this direction ought not be forgotten: 'and all these things shall be yours without the asking' (ibid). There have always been, and always will be, in the Church men who strive with all their might for evangelical perfection and yet in no way fail to be useful to society. Indeed it is the example of their courageous lives and charitable undertakings which fosters and develops the noblest elements in human society.

Since Christian doctrine bears upon all the varied spheres of human acitivity, individual, domestic and social, it is first and foremost necessary that the Church should not deviate from the sacred heritage of truth received from the Fathers. But at the same time she must look to the present, to the new conditions and forms of life in the modern world which have opened up new avenues for the Catholic apostolate.

For this reason the Church has not watched unmoved the wonderful progress in the discoveries of human genius, and has not failed to appreciate their true worth. But as she follows the course of these developments, she does not

fail to remind men to pass beyond material things and look
to God, the source of all wisdom and beauty, never for-
getting that weighty commandment: 'Thou shalt worship
the Lord thy God, and serve none but him' (Matt. 4:10;
Luke 4:8) so that the fleeting fascination of visible things
may not impede true progress.

Different ways of transmitting sacred doctrine.

In the light of the above, it is clear what we should
expect from the Council with regard to doctrine. The 21st
Ecumenical Council which can draw on a fund of such
useful research in the juridical, liturgical, apostolic and
administrative spheres, intends to transmit in its purity
and its integrity the doctrine that in the course of twenty
centuries has become the common heritage of all men. Not
all men willingly accept it, and yet it is a source of enrichment always held out to men of good will.

Our duty, however, is not only to guard this treasure
as though we were only concerned with the past; we have
to give ourselves, resolutely and without fear, to the task
set us by the age we live in, and thus carry on the work
pursued by the Church for twenty centuries.

The essential purpose of the Council, therefore, is not
to discuss this or that article of the Church's fundamental
doctrine, a discussion which is bound to be mainly a re-
production of the teaching of the Fathers and theologians
ancient and modern, which we may presume to be known
and familiar already.

That sort of thing would not, in any case, require a
Council. All over the world the Christian mind, Catholic
and apostolic, out of its renewed, confident and calm ad-

herence to the whole teaching of the Church in all its fullness and precision as it has shone in conciliar decrees from
Trent to Vatican I, is awaiting a leap forward in the direction of doctrinal insight and the formation of a consciousness that will be more perfectly and more faithfully at one
with the authentic doctrine of the Church. That doctrine,
however, needs to be studied and expounded according to
modern disciplines of research and presentation. The sub-
stance of the ancient doctrine, contained in the 'deposit of
faith', is one thing: its formulation is quite another; *that*
depends, for its structure and harmony, upon the needs of
the magisterium whose main function is that of the pastoral
ministry.

Mercy, not harshness.

Today, when the second ecumenical Vatican Council is
about to begin, the fact that the truth of the Lord is everlasting is more than ever apparent. For, as age follows age,
we watch human opinions succeed each other, contradict
each other, and it frequently happens that an error has
barely been proclaimed before it vanishes like mist in sun-
shine.

The Church has always opposed these errors: she has
often condemned them with extreme severity. But today,
the Bride of Christ wishes to heal with mercy rather than
harshness. She considers that the way to answer to modern
needs is to show the value of her teaching rather than
condemn anew. This is not because false doctrines, dangerous opinions and ideas are no longer current, to be guarded
against and dispelled. But rather, they are so obviously
opposed to the norms of common rectitude and lead to

such disastrous results that men seem led to condemn them spontaneously and in particular to reject any way of life that despises God and his law, any excessive reliance on technical progress, any search for well-being that rests only on an easy life. There is a steadily growing conviction in the supreme value of the dignity of the human person, the importance of its progress to perfection, and of the necessary effort this involves. What is more, men have learnt from experience that violence done to others, strength of arms and political domination provide no successful solution to the grave problems that distress them.

In these circumstances, the Catholic Church, by raising aloft the torch of religious truth by means of this Council, hopes to show that she is the loving mother of all men, good, patient, full of compassion and kindliness towards those separated from her. To the human race, burdened with so many difficulties, she repeats Peter's words to the poor man who asked for alms: 'I have no silver and gold but I give you what I have; in the name of Jesus Christ of Nazareth, walk' (Acts 3:6). The Church does not offer impotent wealth to modern man; she does not hold out the hope of mere earthly happiness; she invites men to share in the gifts of divine grace which by raising them to the dignity of the children of God guarantees a more truly human life for them and provides the best means of attaining it. She opens the floodgates of life-giving teaching, enabling them to understand what they really are, their great worth and final destiny, and through her children she spreads abroad the immensity of Christian charity which, more than all else, works for the eradication of discord and is the most powerful factor in the promotion of true understanding, a just peace and the brotherhood of all men.

Unity: the threefold supernatural and constructive enlightenment that emanates from it.

The Church's concern to promote and defend the truth springs from the fact that it is God's purpose that 'all men should be saved and be led to recognize the truth' (Tim. 2 : 4), and that men, without the help of the whole of revealed doctrine, cannot obtain lasting and complete unity of mind and heart and that unity with which true peace and eternal salvation are bound up. Unfortunately the whole Christian family has not yet fully achieved this unity in truth.

The Catholic Church therefore feels bound to strive for the fulfilment of the great mystery of that unity which Christ, as his hour of sacrifice drew near, so earnestly requested of the Father. The Church feels the calm of true peace in her assurance of being most closely united with that prayer, and she greatly rejoices when she sees its power reaching out and producing the benefits of salvation even for those outside her. Indeed, when we ponder the inner meaning of that unity which Christ so fervently begged for his Church, it seems to shed a light which is threefold, supernatural and constructive : the unity of Catholics among themselves, which must be maintained as an example to the world; the unity of prayer and earnest hope in which those separated from this apostolic see express their longing to be united with it; and the unity in esteem and respect for the Catholic Church which is found in the members of the non-Christian religions. On this point, it is sad to have to realize that the majority of the human race still do not benefit from the well-springs of divine grace which flow in the Church, even though every man coming into this world has been redeemed by the blood of Christ. A saying of St Cyprian is especially applicable to the Church whose light enlightens all things and whose power of supernatural unity is spread abroad for the benefit of all mankind: 'The Church, inundated by divine light, irradiates the whole world, and yet it is from a single centre that her brightness shines everywhere, the unity of her body not being broken. The Church, through her fertility, covers the earth with her branches, her streams irrigate an ever wider area; and yet her head is one, her origin is one, the mother, so abundantly fertile, is one. She has engendered us, fed us from her bosom; it is from her spirit that we live' (*De Catholica Ecclesiae Unitate, 5*).

Document III

The message to the world from the Second Vatican Council

On the initiative of bishops from several countries and with the pope's approval, Cardinals Liénart, Doepfner, Léger, Alfrink, Montini, among others, with the help of theologians, composed the message to the world given below. It was read in Latin to the general Congregation of 21 October and after a pause for reflection, it was adopted by the assembly.

TO ALL MEN AND ALL NATIONS WE WISH TO SEND A message of salvation, love and peace which Jesus Christ, son of the living God, brought to the world and entrusted to his Church.

This is why, gathered together in response to the call of His Holiness Pope John XXIII, 'united in prayer with Mary, Mother of Jesus', we, successors of the Apostles, are here assembled in the unity of the apostolic body, of whom the successor of Peter is the head.

In this assembly, under the guidance of the Holy Spirit, our purpose is to seek how we can renew ourselves so that we 'may be found increasingly faithful to the Gospel of Christ'. We shall try to present to the men of our time God's truth in all its integrity and purity in a way that will be intelligible to them and to which they may honestly adhere.

As pastors, we want to meet the needs of all those who are looking for God 'in the hope of somehow finding him and, indeed, he is not far from any one of us'.

This is why, in obedience to the will of Christ who delivered himself to death 'in order to present a Church without spot or wrinkle, holy and without blemish', we shall give ourselves entirely to that work of spiritual renewal, so that the Church, as much through her leaders as through her members, may present to the world the compelling face of Christ who shines in our hearts 'so that the knowledge of God's glory may be resplendent'.

We believe that the Father so loved the world that he gave his son to save it, to deliver us from sin and its bondage, 'to reconcile us with his Father, establishing peace, through the blood of his cross', so that we may be 'sons of God in name and reality'. From his Father's side he sent us his spirit so that we may live from his divine life in love for God and our brethren, forming a single body in Christ.

But we have not the least intention of shirking our tasks in this world; our union with Christ in faith, our hope and love, commit us wholly to the service of our brethren, following the example of our adorable Master 'who came not to be served, but to serve'. That is why the Church was not created to dominate, but to serve. 'He gave his life for us. We must therefore in turn give our lives for our brethren.'

We look, moreover, to the labours of the Council to give a greater brilliancy to the light of faith and so to promote a spiritual renewal and, by repercussion, a fresh impulse that will work to the benefit of the things men prize: scientific discovery, technological progress, and the diffusion of culture.

We bring with us from every part of the earth the material and spiritual distress, the sufferings and aspirations of the peoples entrusted to us. We are alive to the problems which assail them. We wish to include in our care the needs of the humblest, the poorest, the weakest. Like Christ, we are moved to compassion at the sight of the multitudes who suffer from hunger, wretchedness and ignorance. We feel our solidarity with all those who, from the absence of adequate mutual aid, have not yet been able to reach that stage of development which human nature demands.

Also, in our work, we mean to give an important place to all those earthly problems which concern the dignity of man and an authentic community of nations. For 'the love of Christ urges us': 'if anyone sees his brother in need and steels his heart against him, how can the love of God be in him?'

In his broadcast message of 11 September 1962, the supreme pontiff John XXIII emphasized two points in particular.

First the problem of peace between nations. Who does not hold war in horror? Who does not long with his whole soul for peace? The Church shares this feeling, for she is the Mother of all men. Through the voice of the popes, she constantly proclaims her love of peace, her resolution to achieve peace, her full support of every sincere effort to procure it. Is not our assembly in Council itself a living testimony, the visible sign of a community of fraternal love that includes racial, national and linguistic differences?

We affirm the fraternal union of all men, beyond all frontiers and civilizations.

Secondly, the pope recalled the demands of social justice. The doctrine given in *Mater et Magistra* demonstrates that in the modern world it is more necessary than ever for the Church to denounce injustices and crying inequalities, to restore the true hierarchy of values, to make life more human and more in conformity with the principles of the gospel.

Granted, we possess neither economic means nor earthly power; but we place our hope in the power of the spirit which the Lord Jesus promised his Church. That is why, humbly and fervently, we appeal to our brethren whom we serve as pastors, and also to all our brethren who believe in Christ and to all men of good will 'whom God wishes to save and to lead to a knowledge of the truth': may they join with us in working to build themselves a more just and more fraternal earthly city. For it is certainly God's purpose that, through charity, the Kingdom of God may in some way shine out on earth as a remote reflection of his everlasting kingdom.

In a world which is still so far from the peace it longs for, torn by anxiety before the threats presented by technical progress, admirable in itself but perilous when it takes no account of a higher moral law, may the light of great hope in Jesus Christ, the one Saviour of mankind, shine out.

Document IV

On devotion to St Joseph

W HEN OUR REMARKS ON SOME OF THE FORMS OR
developments of the devotion to St Joseph[1] first
appeared they provoked several letters of protest, including one or two that were insulting, and also a criticism from
a lay collaborator of the *Osservatore Romano*, M. Federico
Alessandrini (in the issue of 8 December, 1962). May we
put it on record here that we have neither criticized the
insertion of St Joseph's name in the Canon of the Mass
nor attacked devotion to him.

In fact we were brought up in this devotion, and have
not relaxed it in any way. But with this, as with so many
things, *quando factus sum vir, evacuavi quae erant par-
vuti*, now I am a man, I have put away childish things
(1 Cor. 12:11). This transition from childhood to
maturity has chiefly meant a transition from what was
merely sentimental, more or less human, to an understanding of the economy of salvation derived from Scripture.
We see St Joseph in the context of the faith of the patriarchs, the context described in the eleventh chapter of the
epistle to the Hebrews, and in that sense we have no difficulty in saying: 'It was by faith that Joseph took Mary as

[1] Cf. above, pp. 47-9.

his wife, although he realized she was with child from the Holy Spirit'. It was by faith that he watched over the human life and the earliest experiences of the Word of God made flesh. . . . But even this, great as it is, far from exhausts what we could and would like to say about St Joseph: it would take very little effort to fill a whole book on the subject.

We have set down the theological reasons for reserve and vigilance with regard to certain aspects and forms of devotion to St Joseph, as these have tended to develop, especially since the nineteenth century. We are aware that the devotion itself goes back much earlier than this; to the last years of the fourteenth century when its context was extremely human, and then to the sixteenth century in a deeper and more spiritual context. But in the nineteenth century the devotion acquired a collective element and social aspects. In this way it came to be linked with what we have called devotional ultramontanism, which we consider to have theological and even ecclesiological import, which deserves studying as a whole.

Certain publications and organized institutes today tend to force devotion to St Joseph into the paths taken by the cult of Mary and to apply to it similar categories. For instance, I have before me a *Theology of St Joseph,* in an Italian translation: in it there is a lengthy discussion on St Joseph as belonging to the 'hypostatic order', on his 'fullness of grace', on his resurrection (with the bodies 'of the saints that slept' mentioned in Matt. 27: 52), and even, believe it or not, on his assumption. . . . The pastoral vigilance of the Church does not appear to be disposed to give much encouragement to the attempt to transfer to St Joseph without qualification the privileges that are ad-

mitted for the Mother of God: on 28 April, 1876, the Holy
Office prohibited the use of an *Ave Joseph* which imitated
the *Ave Maria*. We would also recommend the perusal of
the letter of Mgr Harscouet, bishop of Chartres, against
certain excesses in the cults of St Joseph (cf. *Les questions
liturgiques et paroissiales*, August 1931, pp. 208-210).

The comments set down earlier, too brief for so important a subject, proposed as a principle for right judgment
and proper balance, that central thesis of Pauline
theology which St Peter also expressed as follows: 'In his
mortal nature he was done to death, but endowed with
fresh life in his spirit' (Peter 3:18; cf. Rom. 1:14). Of
course the Christ of Easter is identical with the Christ of
Christmas. Of course Christians have much to gain from
imitating Jesus not only in his Passion, but in his life as a
whole, even in his home and hidden life: the mysteries of
Nazareth and those of the Holy Family have much to offer,
and some are specially called to continue their example
(e.g. Fr de Foucauld. . . .). In the spirit and the context
of a soundly balanced Christianity these mysteries of Jesus'
life in the flesh have their hallowed place. All we have done
is to utter a word of warning: these, and still less the
humble, silent St Joseph, are not the things that should
become central. The Christian faith, the Christian religion,
like the liturgical year, have one centre only, the paschal
mystery of Christ.

On this issue there can be no question of allowing simple
folk to fall back on a kind of marginal religion, which has a
greater appeal to the senses and emotions, and is more
human in character. We find the implication of Federico
Allessandrini in the title of his article: *Poor little old
woman*! . . .: totally unacceptable. As if the little old

woman, the *vetula* who was commonplace in the Middle Ages, was incapable of reaching up to the essential message of the Apostles, as if the Gospel was too difficult, too intellectual, for her! We completely reject the idea, which is too often put forward, that a religion grounded in Scripture is a possibility for developed and cultivated minds alone, and that simple folk should be directed to devotions that appeal to the senses.

We urge nothing against devotions, so long as they keep their place. Catholicism is a religion in which the Lord is really present, and he is never without his saints. Any mystery of Christ deprived of its radiation in the saints would be light without warmth, a hearth without heat. But experience warns us to be on the lookout for a possible danger. In religion, as in other matters, space is in practice limited and our powers of attention have their saturation point. If exuberant development and over-emphatic emphasis are allowed to those devotions which satisfy man's religious instinct only too well or to a cult of the Mother of God that is less Christological than instinctively human or even to the human aspects of the earthly life of Jesus Christ, then all these things, which do have their place in the most authentic traditional Christianity, will be found, *in practice,* to have taken up all the available room. The exercise of these devotions, with their corresponding emotions and literature, will *in fact* come to constitute the religious life. The centre may well continue *in theory* to be the paschal mystery of Christ, but *in practice* that position will have been occupied by devotions, in the life of the people, in the activities of their pastors, and even in the practical questions such as the lay-out of churches and the organization of worship.

It is against distortions of this kind, and against these alone, that we have protested. We assert, in the most definite way, as the result of experience gained chiefly outside France, that this distortion and danger are not simply figments of our imagination!

Document V

Closing speech of John XXIII at the conclusion of the First Session 8 December, 1962

THE FIRST SESSION OF THE COUNCIL CAME TO AN END on 8 December. It was feared that the pope's illness might prevent him from taking part in the ceremony. He was, however, both able and willing to come to the basilica of St Peter, and he himself gave a summary of the results of this first session, emphasizing as he did so all that remains to be done, all that is to be hoped for. Below we reproduce almost the whole of his speech.

An act of faith in God.

The Council—in its reality—is an act of faith in God, of obedience to his laws, of sincere striving to fit ourselves to the plan of redemption, in accordance with which the Word became flesh through the Virgin Mary. And since at this time we are venerating 'the stainless branch of the root of Jesse' through whom its flower came to us (*flos de radice evius ascendet*), our hearts are filled with an immense joy, especially as this flower is revealed to us in the light of Advent.

Now that the bishops of five continents are about to leave this council hall to return to their beloved dioceses, to carry on their service as pastors leading their flocks, the mind likes to dwell on what has been done up to now so as to get a sense of direction and food for encouragement. It is refreshing to take a look at the future, anticipating what still remains to be done in order that this great enterprise may be brought to a successful conclusion.

Our survey will bear upon the three following points: the opening of the Ecumenical Council; its continuation; the results we may expect from it for the radiation of faith, holiness and the apostolate in the Church and in our present society.

The first session summed up.

We find it impossible to forget the opening of the Ecumenical Council. We still see that great gathering of bishops from the entire Catholic world, unique so far in history. The Church, one, holy, catholic and apostolic, came before mankind in the splendour of her eternal mission, in her unshakeable construction, in the persuasive strength and attraction of her varied forms of life. We also like to recall the delegations that came from a number of nations to represent the governments of their countries and to take part in the solemn inauguration of the Council. With reference to this, we wish once again to express our gratitude for the fact that the entire world has been enabled to feel the wonder of this opening, and for the evidence of a truly extraordinary interest which has reached us from all over the world, with unanimous expressions of respect, esteem and gratitude.

After that unforgettable 11 October the work of the Council began, and at the end of this first session it is natural to draw certain timely conclusions.

The first session has been as it were a slow and solemn introduction to the main activity of the Council, a disinterested attempt to discover what God really wants. It was necessary for brethren coming from afar and assembled at the same centre to renew contacts so as to establish better mutual understanding. Each had to meet the other's eyes; each had to feel the beating of his brother's heart. They needed to pool their varied experiences, to exchange, for the sake of profitable reflection, the facts of pastoral administration in apostolates of the most widely differing mentalities and cultures.

In so vast a body, it will also be appreciated that it took some days to reach agreement on matters about which, whilst observing charity, there were easily understandable differences of view and some apprehension. These providential discussions enabled the truth to be elucidated, and they allowed the world to witness the sacred freedom of the Sons of God as it exists in the Church.

It was not an accident that work began with the Schema on the Liturgy: man's relations with God. These relations belong to the highest order of reality: if the welfare of souls is to be served, they should be established on the firm foundation of Revelation and the apostolic magisterium, with that breadth of vision that should concede nothing to ease or haste, as sometimes happens in relations between human beings.

Five other Schemas were presented, and these alone

suffice to indicate the significance of the work so far done, and to justify the conclusion that there has been achieved a fitting introduction to what still remains to be examined.

The hope that the Council will have finished its work by Christmas, 1963.

And now, Venerable Brethren, we may turn with confidence to that almost silent but no less important stage which, after you have returned to your dioceses, will occupy the nine months' interval.

As we think of each one of you in his own diocese, our heart is filled with warmth; for you know that when you go home from Rome, you will be bringing your Christian people the lighted torch of trust and charity and you will remain united with us in most fervent prayer. This reminds us of the words of Ecclesiasticus about the high priest Simeon: 'He stood at the foot of the altar, compassed with his brethren round about' (Ecclus. 50:13). As you see, our activity will continue in this mutual union of prayer and common purpose.

Today's ceremony, therefore, does not mark a cessation of work; on the contrary, that which remains for us all to do will be of great importance; there has never been anything like it in the intervals of other Councils. In fact, the conditions of modern life greatly facilitate rapid personal and apostolic communication of every kind.

That the work is to go on is shown by the institution of a new Commission, made up of members of the Sacred College and the episcopate, and representing the universal Church. This Commission's duty is to follow and direct the work during these nine months, and along with the various conciliary Commissions to lay the foundations of a successful conclusion of the Ecumenical Council. Thus the Council will remain open during the coming months when ecumenical sessions, in the strict sense, will be suspended.

Each bishop, in spite of the demands made upon by him by his pastoral administration, will continue to study and assimilate the Schemas at his disposal and whatever may be sent to him at suitable times. With this preparation, all the Fathers of the Church, as is their wish, will meet again in Rome. The session that will begin in September will have a well-defined, uninterrupted and speedier rhythm, made possible by these two months of 1962, so that we may even hope to see the conclusions of its labours —eagerly awaited by all the faithful—in the glory of the Incarnation of the Son of God, amidst the joy of Christmas, in the centenary year of the Council of Trent.

Looking down these broad avenues, full of promise for the coming year, makes us yearn from the depth of our heart for the fulfilment of the great purposes which made us decide to call a Council: that 'the Church with a faith stronger than ever, a more determined hope, a more burning charity, may gain new and youthful vigour; that strengthened by the sacred decisions that will be taken, she may be more energetic and more alert in promoting the reign of Christ' (*Autograph letter to the German episcopate*, 11 January, 1961).

A gigantic task of preaching on the part of all pastors.

Even though the stage for applying decisions is not at hand, since this can come only when the work of the

Council has been finally completed, it is nonetheless re-
warding to look forward to the results which seem likely
to ensue: results for the Catholic Church; what we hope
for our brethren who are proud to call themselves Christian; fresh interest on the part of those many men who
are descendants of ancient and glorious civilizations from
which the light of Christianity has no wish to subtract
anything, but rather—as has happened before in history
—hopes to be able to develop the most fruitful seeds of
robust religion and human progress.

Our heart is expectant, Venerable Brethren, and we
know well that yours too are full of the same eager concern, like the watcher in the night who keeps his eyes fixed
on the horizon for the first gleams of dawn.

The thing to do then will be to extend to every sphere
of the Church's life, including those bearing on social questions, the directives of the Council, and of applying them
with 'generous, sincere and assiduous determination'
(prayer for the Ecumenical Council). This most important stage will see the pastors united in a gigantic task of
preaching sound doctrine and of applying the laws they
themselves will have made; and for this work the collaboration of the diocesan and regular clergy, religious orders,
and of the Catholic laity in every sphere and to their full
capability, will be needed, so that what the Fathers have
done may be seconded by the most joyful and loyal
response.

This will indeed be the 'new Pentecost', thanks to which
the interior life of the Church will flourish and her
maternal concern will extend to every section of human
activity. It will be a fresh leap forward for Christ's kingdom
in the world, a fresh proclamation, still more profound

and persuasive, of the joyful news of the Redemption; the clearest statement of God's sovereignty, of human brotherhood in charity, of the peace promised on earth to men of good will, in correspondence with God's grace.

'May this peace go with you!'

These, Venerable Brethren, are the feelings which throng in our heart and are transformed into prayer and hope. Having finished the work of the present session of the Council, you are about to return to your own countries and to the beloved flocks entrusted to you. We wish you a safe journey and at the same time ask you to give our greetings and convey our warmest wishes to your priests and people. We are reminded, in the present circumstances, of words full of encouraging hope spoken by our predecessor Pius IX at the First Vatican Council: 'Behold, Brethren, how good and joyful a thing it is to dwell together in unity in the house of God. May you ever continue in this way. And as our Lord Jesus Christ gave peace to the Apostles, I also, his most unworthy Vicar, give you peace in his name. Peace, as you know, drives out fear; peace seals the ears against baseless talk. May such peace be with you all the days of your life' (*Mansi* 1869–70, p. 765, 156).

During the past months, gathered here together, we have experienced the consoling truth of those words of Pius IX.

A long road still lies ahead, but you know that the Supreme Pastor will follow you with his love in your pastoral work in your respective dioceses, a work that will not be separated from preoccupation with the Council. In pointing out the threefold sphere of activity proposed for our work together we wanted to arouse your enthusiasm; the brilliant initial efforts of the Council have been the introduction to a great undertaking; in the months that follow the common work will be actively continued, in reflection and meditation, so that the Ecumenical Council may bring to the human family the longed for benefits of faith, hope and charity. This threefold characteristic shows the quite special importance of the Council.

Great responsibilities lie upon us, therefore, but God himself will maintain us on our journey.

May the Immaculate Virgin be with us always, may her most chaste husband St Joseph, patron of the Ecumenical Council—whose name will from today shine in the canon of the mass all over the world—be with us on our journey, just as, by God's will, he maintained and supported the Holy Family. And may Saints Peter and Paul, and all the Apostles, and Saint John the Baptist, with the bishops, pastors and doctors of the Church of God also be with you.

We stand now in this basilica of St Peter, at the centre of Christendom, near the tomb of the Prince of the Apostles; but we like to remember that the cathedral of the diocese of Rome is the Lateran basilica 'mother and foundation of all churches', dedicated to Christ, the divine Saviour; to him then who is the immortal and invisible King of all ages and peoples, be glory and power for ever and ever (cf. 1 Tim. 1 : 17; Apoc. 1 : 6).

In this hour of joy and heartfelt feeling heaven seems to open above us, and the radiant splendour of the heavenly court to come down upon us, endowing our hearts with superhuman certitude, a spirit of supernatural faith, joy and profound peace. Inundated by this light and in expectation of the time when you will return, we greet you, Venerable Brethren, and 'we embrace you in the Lord' (cf. Rom. 16:16); we ask that the fullest of divine blessings may be yours, and that the apostolic Blessing be the pledge and the promise of this.

Document VI

The Schema 'On the means of
Social Communication' [1]

THE FATHERS OF THE COUNCIL WERE CONTENT WITH
two and a half general Congregations for the discussion of the problems of the press, radio, cinema and television, which are so important in the modern world and
are such novelties in a council.

On 23 November the Schema *On the Means of Social
Communication* was submitted to the Council for study.
It had been worked out by the 'Secretariat for the Press
and Public Shows' under the direction of Bishop O'Connor
(American), president of the pontifical Commission for
the cinema, radio and television.[2] The discussion was continued on the 24th; it was interrupted on the 25th, which
was a Sunday. On Monday 26 November, at 11.30 (this
was the 27th general Congregation) the assembly unani-

---

[1] This text is the work of Fr Gabel A.A. It is taken from an article in
Témoignage Chrétien, with the author's permission.
[2] The Schema is composed of a preamble and four parts: (a). The
Church's teaching on this subject. (b). The postolate through these
means. (c). The norm of morality applicable to its use. (d). Various
means, discussed individually: press, cinema, radio, television, and a
few others, e.g. gramophone records, tape-recorders, comic papers.

mously voted for the closing of the discussion on the
Schema, following a suggestion from the council of presidency.

This haste was not at all to the taste of Bishop Stourm
(France), an eloquent and competent advocate. For
many years he has been able to evaluate the characteristics
of this factor of our civilization: the instantaneous and
universal imparting of information; the bringing within
the reach of all men and the presence even in the home
of technically fascinating and psychologically contrived
means of culture and influence.

Several Fathers, moreover, had the feeling that the
Council was not sufficiently prepared to be able to give
this Schema the attention it deserved. The official communiqué published on Saturday 24 November (i.e. on the
first day of the discussion) contained, in fact, the following
paragraph: 'Some (Fathers) have expressed the fear that
the Council has not laid sufficient emphasis on the matter
at present being examined, which involves a problem of
vital importance in every form of the modern apostolate.'
This amounts to asking whether for many Fathers the
good or evil usage of these means is of less importance for
the propagation of the gospel than the question of the use
of Latin or the vernacular which had just been discussed
at length. Looking at the different treatment meted out to
these two problems, one is tempted to agree!

There are three reasons which may account for the
brevity of the discussion: the quality of the Schema, the
necessities of the timetable and, especially, the absence of
any theology of the problem.

The doctrinal motivation of the Schema was sound and

its suggestions were practical; thus there was no fundamental disagreement about it. The timetable was partly responsible. After six weeks spent in discussing the Liturgy and the sources of Revelation, many Fathers were worried by the prospect of the first session ending before the two questions which they regarded as being by far the most important had been broached: Christian unity and the status of the episcopate. There was little hope now that they would be investigated thoroughly. But at least a gesture had to be made and essential directives given to the Commissions who were to work between the two sessions.

Defective content: defective competency.

It was this anxiety which partly explains why the Fathers were in such a hurry to end the discussion. But the real explanation lies elsewhere, for even had time not been lacking, the discussion would not have gone on for long, for lack of genuine content and of competence to discuss it.

The hierarchy, with rare exceptions, were unable to realize the real proportions of this phenomenon of civilization; by this I mean that in the Church there is still no scientific appreciation of this phenomenon or, more correctly, what is lacking is *a theological consideration of the implications of the data that are scientifically known.*

For example, the way in which in ecclesiastical circles 'Information', and the press in particular, are spoken about has a curious affinity with the sentimental and romantic style adopted in the same circles seventy-five or even fifty years ago with regard to the social question. It was then believed that the social question could be solved if the poor could be made moral and the rich generous. Since that time a scientific study of economic and social questions has been made, and action taken with regard to the institutions and forms of social life. The same stage must be reached in Catholic circles with regard to 'Information,' the press and all the other mass media.

Knowledge and language are interconnected. A subject is discussed to the extent and according to the way in which it is known. Here is a simple example: with regard to freedom of information, the attitude most usually adopted is a moralizing one, with the risk of a general confusion which blurs the distinctions between different but interrelated aspects of this fundamental problem, aspects that result from differences in techniques, differences in status between the enterprise, the publication (or its content) and the profession.

Personally I know of only one manual of ethics for seminaries which studies the press from any other aspect than that of occasions of sin or scandal. That is the *La Loi du Christ* by Fr Haering. He groups his reflections under the heading: 'The techniques for the dissemination of knowledge, and personal communion in truth and beauty.'

Modern means of disseminating knowledge for the good of mankind.

By an impressive vote of 2138, the Fathers expressed their approval of the general spirit of the Schema, which is positive, optimistic, clearly in line with *Mirandi Prorsus*. To begin with, modern means of communication are a gift from God. They can and must be used for the benefit of mankind in general and preaching of the Gospel in particular.

The vote was significant. This was the first chance the Fathers of the Council had been given to express the spirit in which they meant to approach and judge modern civilization. The Church is not afraid of the world of technology. Certainly she distinguishes between its advantages and its dangers, but she gives confidence to men and to Christians, and she has confidence in them. This is a very different manner of speaking from that used in the Church for a hundred years concerning the press and, at the beginning of the century, concerning the cinema.

The Council also wished for a distinction to be made between fundamental doctrinal positions (the real work of the Council) and practical suggestions (the work of an institution in the Church). The codification and explanation of practical directives could become the business of the pontifical Commission for the cinema, radio and television, which could be extended to include the press (should the pope so decide), as an article in the Schema suggested. This incidentally was the only article on which a separate vote was taken.

The mixture of doctrine with practical suggestions was due to the fact that, in its final version, the Schema aimed at omitting none of the directives given in the recent encyclicals. This anxiety to have the right references, this almost obsequious attitude towards them, definitely prevented the Schema from exploring fresh ground with any courage, from speaking with authority to mankind in general and the professions in particular and from shedding the light of natural ethics, that would meet with universal acceptance, on problems which belong not only to personal morality but to the structure of society.

Document VII

The thirty-nine Observers present at the first session of Vatican II

The Church of England
> Very Rev John Moorman (England) Bishop of Ripon.
> Rev Frederick Grant (United States)
> Venerable Charles de Souza (Ceylon) Bishop of Colombo.

World Lutheran Federation
> Prof Kristin Skydsgaard (Denmark) Professor of Theology, Copenhagen.
> Prof George Linbeck (United States) American theologian.

World Reformed Alliance
> Rev Hébert Roux (France) Reformed Church.
> Rev Douglas Shaw (Scotland) Presbyterian Church.
> Rev James Nichols (United States) Princetown Theological College.

The German Evangelical Church
> Prof Edmund Schlink (Germany) University of Heidelberg.

World Convention of the Churches of Christ (disciples of Christ)

> Rev Jesse Bader (United States) Secretary general of the convention.

The World Committee of Quakers

> Rev Richard Ullmann (Great Britain)

World Council of Congregationalists

> Rev Douglas Horton (United States)
>
> Prof George B. Caird (Great Britain) Mansfield College, Oxford.

World Council of Methodists

> Bishop Fred. Corson (United States) President of the World Council.
>
> Dr Harold Roberts (Great Britain) Principal of Richmond Theological College.
>
> Dr Albert Outler (United States) Professor of theology at Dallas.

World Council of Churches

> Pastor Lukas Vischer (Switzerland) Reformed Church.

Old Catholic Church (Union of Utrecht)

> Canon Peter Maan (Holland) Professor in the Seminary of Amersfoort.

Coptic Church

> Fr Youanna Girgis (United Arab Republics) Minister of Public Instruction.
>
> Dr Mikhail Tadros (Counsellor of the Appeal Court).

Syro-Jacobite Church

> Fr Raman Zakkan B. Iwas (Syria).
>
> Fr Paul Verghese (Syria).

Orthodox Church of Egypt
    Abbé Petros Gabre Selassie.
    Dr Chebre Sadeque.

Armenian Church
    Fr Vardoet Karkin Surkassian.

Baptist National Convention of the United States
    Dr J. Jackson

International Association of Liberal Christianity
    Prof Van Hock (Holland) University of Leyden.
    Prof Adams (United States) University of Harvard.
    Pastor Greely (United States).

European Exarchate of the Russian Orthodox Church (does not recognize the patriarchate of Moscow, but that of Constantinople)
    Mgr Antoine (Switzerland).
    The Archpriest Igor Troyanoff (Switzerland) of Lausanne.

Russian Orthodox Church
    Patriarchate of Moscow
    Archpriest Vitaly Borovoï (U.S.S.R.) the representative of the Russian Orthodox Church at the World Council of Churches.
    Archpriest Vladimir Kocliarov (U.S.S.R.) Vice president of the Orthodox mission in Jerusalem.

Personally invited by the Secretariat for Unity
    Prof G. C. Berkhouwer (Holland) Reformed Dutch Protestant, University of Amsterdam.
    Canon Bernard Pawley (Great Britain) Church of England, Ely Cathedral.
    Fr Alexander Schmemann (United States) St Wladimir's Seminary, New York.

Prof Oscar Cullmann, Universities of Basle, Stras-
bourg and Paris.
Pastor Schütz (France) Prior of Taizé.
Pastor Thurian (France) Sub-Prior of Taizé.